Cambridge Elements ☰

Elements in Politics and Society in Southeast Asia
edited by
Edward Aspinall
Australian National University
Meredith L. Weiss
University at Albany, SUNY

CAMBODIA

Return to Authoritarianism

Kheang Un
Northern Illinois University

I0957294

🛡 **CAMBRIDGE**
UNIVERSITY PRESS

CAMBRIDGE
UNIVERSITY PRESS

University Printing House, Cambridge CB2 8BS, United Kingdom

One Liberty Plaza, 20th Floor, New York, NY 10006, USA

477 Williamstown Road, Port Melbourne, VIC 3207, Australia

314–321, 3rd Floor, Plot 3, Splendor Forum, Jasola District Centre,
New Delhi – 110025, India

79 Anson Road, #06–04/06, Singapore 079906

Cambridge University Press is part of the University of Cambridge.

It furthers the University's mission by disseminating knowledge in the pursuit of
education, learning, and research at the highest international levels of excellence.

www.cambridge.org
Information on this title: www.cambridge.org/9781108457934
DOI: 10.1017/9781108558648

© Kheang Un 2019

First published 2019

A catalogue record for this publication is available from the British Library.

ISBN 978-1-108-45793-4 Paperback
ISSN 2515-2998 (online)
ISSN 2515-298X (print)

Cambodia

Return to Authoritarianism

Elements in Politics and Society in South East Asia

DOI: 10.1017/9781108558648
First published online: February 2019

Abstract: Drawing data from multiple sources, Un argues that following the 1993 United Nations intervention to promote democracy, the Cambodian People's Party (CPP) perpetuated a patronage state weak in administrative capacity but strong in coercive capacity. This enabled them to maintain the presence of electoral authoritarianism, but increased political awareness among the public, the rise in political activism among community-based organizations, and a united opposition led to the emergence of a counter-movement. Sensing that this counter-movement might be unstoppable, the CPP has returned Cambodia to authoritarianism, a move made possible in part by China's pivot to Cambodia.

Keywords: Cambodia, democratization, civil society, China's influence, electoral authoritarianism

ISBNs: 9781108457934 (PB) 9781108558648 (OC)
ISSNs: 2515-2998 (online) 2515-298X (print)

Contents

1 Introduction

Cambodia was the site of a Cold War proxy conflict beginning as a "side show" to the Vietnam War in the 1960s and 1970s (Shawcross, 1981) and subsequently as a zone for Sino–Soviet and US–Soviet rivalry that prolonged a civil war in Cambodia until the 1990s (Chanda, 1986; Chandler, 2008). The end of the Cold War paved the way for a comprehensive political settlement known as the Paris Peace Agreement (PPA) that had the twin objectives of rebuilding Cambodia's economy and inaugurating a liberal democratic political system. Under the terms of the PPA, the United Nations Transitional Authority in Cambodia (UNTAC) oversaw a democratic transition through multi-party elections and the drafting of a liberal constitution in 1992–1993 (Heder and Legerwood, 1996).

Since elections in 1993, the international community – through overseas development assistance (ODA) – has continued to promote Cambodia's economy and democracy. Despite these international efforts, Cambodia's democracy has gained little traction. For the most part since 1993, Cambodia's democracy could be characterized as electoral authoritarianism,[1] wherein multi-party elections occurred but the elections were neither free nor fair, and civil and political liberties were curtailed. It is important to note that electoral authoritarian regimes are not static. The level of competition in authoritarian regimes can vary contingent on the levels of popular political awareness and the unity of opposition camps and Western leverage and linkages (Levitsky and Way, 2010). By 2017, Cambodia's electoral authoritarianism regressed into hegemonic electoral authoritarianism;[2] in 2018, the ruling Cambodian People's Party (CPP) orchestrated an election with its main opponent – the Cambodian National Rescue Party (CNRP) – outlawed.

Cambodia: Return to Authoritarianism draws on multiple sources of data including longitudinal field research that includes interviews with multiple stakeholders, such as party apparatchik, leaders of civil society organizations, farmers, and representatives of bilateral and multilateral institutions operating in Cambodia to trace the social and political changes that account for political dynamics in post-UNTAC Cambodia. First, it argues that despite Western efforts at promoting a rational-legal state that would help strengthen democracy, the CPP perpetuated a state dominated by clientelism and rent-seeking, producing a government with weak administrative capacity but strong in coercive capability. Second, as a means to gain access to international assistance and trade, the CPP permitted the presence of some semblance of

---

[1] For discussion of the concept see Schedler (2006).
[2] For discussion of the concept see Diamond (2002).

democracy while using its control over a patronage-based state to coopt and coerce opposition parties and civil society organizations and to influence voters. Third, socio-economic changes galvanized popular political awareness, uniting the opposition to rally for leadership change. Sensing that a counter-movement might be unstoppable under electoral authoritarianism, the CPP returned Cambodia to authoritarianism, the return made partly possible by China's pivot to Cambodia, which provides the CPP with a cushion against Western pressure.

The analysis begins by tracing the development of the Cambodian state, arguing that despite formal trappings of democracy and a modern bureaucratic system, the state is dominated by informal elements of patron-clientelism. These conditions result in a weak state in terms of administrative capacity, service provision, and ability to curb corruption. However, the Cambodian state is strong in terms of coercive capacity, as Cambodian leaders politicized the security forces. The ruling party employs units supposedly designed for inter-institutional accountability namely the judiciary, the Constitutional Council, and the National Assembly as tools to suppress democratic forces and popular democratic aspirations. One of the apparent weaknesses of the Cambodian state is manifested by its hobbled and politicized judiciary. The logic of authoritarianism is that the ruling party does not allow the judiciary to serve as an effective institution of horizontal accountability that can check potential abuses of power by the ruling elite. Consequently, any judicial reform tends to promote "rule by law" or "weaponizing laws" rather than rule of law. The networks of political and economic elites selectively deploy a politicized judiciary to suppress political opposition and civil society groups and to promote their interests.

The book then addresses how weak state capacity associated with entrenched neo-patrimonialism limits the government's ability to control corruption and mobilize resources for the public good. The next section analyzes political parties, elections, and civil society under electoral authoritarianism. It argues that, as elections are the source of domestic and international legitimacy, the ruling party allows multi-party elections and civil society to be present; however, it uses both threats and material inducements to ensure electoral victory. The extent of the ruling party's use of each element depends on the scope of the challenge posed by the opposition and civil society. Cambodia's weak state means that public service provisions in terms of education, healthcare, and infrastructure, such as rural roads and bridges, are poor. With these conditions in play, the ruling party utilizes patronage resources mobilized from business tycoons and government-cum-party officials to project itself as an indispensable force for Cambodia.

Despite the party's initial success in attracting voters, the CPP's patronage politics produces contradictions. On the one hand, while permitting the party to dispense resources to build local infrastructure, CPP's patronage politics has spawned corruption and expropriation of the country's resources by politically well-connected groups resulting in increased inequality and social injustice.

Over time, as the next section highlights, Cambodia's social and economic changes, such as a bulge in the youth population, the availability of social media, and migration to urban areas by employment seekers, have broadened popular awareness of the adverse effects of the CPP's patronage politics. These developments led to the growth of counter-movements challenging the status quo. The most significant recent push-back was the merger of the two major opposition parties – the Sam Rainsy Party (SRP) and the Human Rights Party (HRP) – into a united Cambodia National Rescue Party (CNRP) in 2012. The rise of counter-movements also emerged from increased political activism within Cambodian civil society. The United Nations' intervention in 1993 gave birth to non-governmental organizations (NGOs), which grew with ongoing international political and financial support.

These NGOs were initially seen as synonymous with civil society, yet were largely devoid of linkages with the masses. However, by the early 2000s, Cambodia's socio-economic transformation had heightened popular awareness of social and political injustice arising from the ravages of crony-capitalism and electoral authoritarianism. These socio-economic changes, compounded by NGOs adapting strategies linking them to people at the community level, gave birth to a new genre of civil society groups: community-based organizations (CBOs). In the meantime, key progressive trade unions became more vocal over the years in their demands for higher wages and better working conditions. To achieve their objectives these unions rallied behind the opposition parties. They organized strikes and participated in demonstrations against electoral irregularities. In short, unified opposition forces coupled with greater political awareness resulted in counter-movements that called for state institutional reform, social justice, and deeper democracy.

Following the 2013 national elections, the CPP was aware of increased popular discontent toward the government and attempted some reforms. However, given entrenched patronage and corruption, any drastic and meaningful reforms were impossible. By 2017, the ruling party believed that the opposition might be unstoppable if the CPP allowed the continuation of electoral authoritarianism with the presence of a united opposition party, press freedom (albeit limited), and the rather open operation of civil society organizations. Consequently, as the final section discusses, the CPP used the legislature it controls to pass laws restricting the operation of civil society organizations and political parties. The ruling party eventually deployed the constrained and politicized judiciary to dismantle the CNRP. The ruling party also closed down independent media outlets. The CPP's decisions to increase its authoritarian tendencies can be attributed partly to global geo-political shifts. The mirage of Cambodia's democracy since its inception had persisted in part due to Western pressure. Over time, Western leverage declined, further precipitated by President Donald Trump's America First Doctrine. Amidst this declining Western leverage, China pivoted to Cambodia, providing the latter with financial assistance, sources of foreign investment, and market access. The trend in Cambodia toward hegemonic electoral authoritarianism emerged following an election in July 2018 without the presence of the main opposition party – the CNRP.

KEY POLITICAL PARTIES IN CAMBODIA

CPP: Cambodian People's Party

The then ruling People's Revolutionary Party of Kampuchea in 1989 changed its name to the Cambodian People's Party to dissociate the party from its communist past and affiliation with the Vietnamese occupation of Cambodia (1979–1989). Although the CPP no longer adheres to Marxist-Leninism, its administrative structure contains key characteristics of a communist party i.e., the affinity between the party and the state. The CPP, headed by Hun Sen, has maintained control over Cambodia since 1993; the basis for their support is claiming credit for victory over the genocidal Khmer Rouge regime, and economic growth and stability. By banning its main rival – the CNRP – the CPP captured all of the 125 National Assembly seats, transforming Cambodia from electoral authoritarianism to hegemonic electoral authoritarianism in 2018.

FUNCINPEC: National United Front for an Independent, Neutral, Peaceful and Cooperative Cambodia

A royalist party emerging from an armed movement against the Vietnamese occupation of Cambodia. Led by Prince Norodom Rannaridh, son of former King Norodom Sihanouk, FUNCINPEC won the most seats in the UN-sponsored elections in 1993. Serving nominally as senior partner from 1993–1997, it became a junior coalition partner in the CPP-led government from 1998 to early 2005. Renewed internal conflicts led to the ousting of Prince Ranariddh as its president in 2006. With the help of Hun Sen, Ranariddh became once again president of

FUNCINPEC in 2015. Lack of a concrete policy platform and ineffective leadership meant FUNCINPEC became politically irrelevant.

SRP: Sam Rainsy Party
An opposition party founded by Sam Rainsy as an offshoot of the Khmer Nation Party (KNP) which he also founded following his dismissal from FUNCINPEC and the National Assembly in 1995. Victim of CPP's divide and rule tactics, the KNP split into a pro-CPP faction and the Sam Rainsy faction. Following a protracted legal fight in the CPP controlled courts, Sam Rainsy founded the SRP in 1998. SRP supported liberal democracy and Western style capitalism. Its initial base came from textile workers and urban merchants; drawn by the SRP's fierce attacks on government corruption and social injustice.

HRP: Human Rights Party
An opposition party founded by Kem Sokha, former Director of the Cambodian Center for Human Rights (CCHR). While at CCHR, Kem organized village meetings and public forums to promote democracy, human rights, social justice, and the fight against corruption. Gaining name recognition from these campaigns, Kem founded HRP in 2007 based on the principles of liberal democracy.

CNRP: Cambodia National Rescue Party
Formed from the merger in 2012 between SRP and HRP, CNRP was the largest, most popular, and best organized opposition party. CNRP built strength from HRP's rural base and SRP's urban base. CNRP's political platform was based on liberal democracy and capitalism, populism, and nationalism. CNRP's electoral strength rivaled that of the CPP in 2013 national elections and 2017 local elections; the CPP dissolved it ahead of the 2018 national elections. Its leader, Kem Sokha, was arrested in 2017 and imprisoned for a year. In September 2018, the government released him from jail but continues to hold him under house arrest.

GDP: Grassroots Democracy Party
The party was founded by rural development specialist Yang Saing Koma and social commentator Kem Ley. Kem's assassination in 2016 was broadly believed to be linked to his outspokenness against the government. GDP's core political platform seeks term limits for public office holders and effective resource management. It first contested the 2017 local elections when it won the majority of seats in five out of 11,572 commune councils.

2 Patronage, Power, and the State

The international community through the Paris Peace Agreement (PPA) attempted to implant a rational legal state in Cambodia. However, the presence of a neo-patrimonial system at the time of the introduction of democracy overshadowed such efforts at state building. Cambodia's neo-patrimonial state possesses two elements: (1) formal political institutions such as a constitution, government institutions, political parties, and security forces; and (2) informal networks of patron-clientelism. Formal state institutions serve as focal points for external relations, including government contacts with bilateral and multi-lateral institutions and mechanisms for the ruling elites/party to exercise control over both coercive and economic resources that, in John Sidel's words (1997: 961), are made possible by "state-based derivative and discretionary power." Behind the façade of formal state institutions lay networks of patron-clientelism that constitute, to use Chabal and Daloz's phrase (1999: xix) a "realm of the informal, uncodified and unpoliced" politics which are predominant, serving as the true foundation for political and economic powers. The ruling CPP had used a neo-patrimonial state since 1993 to project electoral authoritarianism and when that order appeared unsustainable, the Cambodian People's Party (CPP) then returned Cambodia to hegemonic electoral authoritarianism.

Although patron-clientelism is embedded in a polity's social, economic, and political structure, it is a dynamic institution, transforming itself in response to changes in domestic and international economics and politics. In the era of globalization, patronage resources and networks are increasingly and intricately tied to external economic actors. Through patron-clientelism native entrepreneurs connect government institutions and officials to foreign capitalists in web-like networks. These multi-faceted and multi-layered forms of interactions offer patronage networks new opportunities for collusion, producing new patterns of resource extraction and political and economic domination. Furthermore, neo-patrimonial networks also undergo transformation when countries embark on democratization, either through exogenous or endogenous pressures. Public and private spheres are blurred, and state officials, in many cases, consider state assets or resources as their own. Under these conditions, to use Chabal and Daloz's phrase (1999: 2-5), "the substance of politics is to be found in the myriad networks" that connect various layers of power.

2.1 The Evolution of Patron-clientelism

State structure and capacity in contemporary Cambodia are understandably intertwined with the country's historical, political, and economic developments.

French colonial rule established a "modern state" in Cambodia, which was strong in terms of its extractive capacity but weak in other areas. Upon gaining independence from France in 1953, the Cambodian state continued to be weak. Reliant on his personal charisma and the notion of semi-divinity, King (and after 1955 Prince) Norodom Sihanouk embodied the nation and therefore effectively blocked any institutionalization of the state (Osborne, 1994; Leifer, 1968). The effects of the Vietnam War and the ensuing civil war in the 1970s further weakened the Cambodian state (Shawcross, 1981; Chandler, 2008). More devastating were the near total destruction of state institutions and society, the massacre of educated Cambodians by Pol Pot's ultra-Maoist regime (1975–1979) (Chandler, 1991; Kiernan, 2002), and the subsequent civil war and international embargo of the Vietnam-backed People's Republic of Kampuchea (PRK, 1979–1989) (Gottesman, 2003). It has taken an entire generation for Cambodian society to recover from the ghastly legacy of war and genocide. Fear of a return to violence haunts the generation who survived this horrific period.

It should be noted that the contemporary Cambodian state's structure and capacity evolved, for the most part, from the period of the PRK and the State of Cambodia (SoC, 1989–1993). Despite the promulgation of a new liberal constitution and a coalition government following the United Nations' intervention in 1993, the CPP – which has its roots in the People's Revolutionary Party of Kampuchea that controlled Cambodia from 1979 to 1989) – continued to dominate the state thereafter. The CPP domination of the Cambodian state is anchored on the party's "interlocking pyramids of patron-client networks" (Heder, 1995: 425).

These networks, which Cambodians call *ksae* or "string," are in constant competition for supremacy, or cooperate at a minimum, to maintain the status quo. These networks are linked to two other elements: corruption and the use of force in a mutually reinforcing triangular mechanism. This mechanism impacts various dimensions of state capacity and democratic development through their reinforcement of "interminable vicious circles" (Putnam, Leonardi and Nanetti, 1994).

Through these *ksae*, officials at local, provincial, and national levels exercise personal control over the state apparatus, through which they and their clients monopolize a variety of economic activities through the non-transparent issuance of licenses, contracts, and permits in addition to siphoning resources from the state budget. In contemporary Cambodia, the networks that have a high impact on political and economic transformations are found within the ruling CPP. Within the CPP, up until the early 2000s, there existed two competing supra-networks: the Chea Sim/Sar Kheng network and the Hun Sen network, both of which originated in the 1980s and evolved throughout the years of civil war. Chea Sim, from 1979 until his death in 2015, held powerful portfolios within the government and party including Minister of Interior, President of the CPP, President of the National Assembly, and President of the Senate. In the1980s, due to his skillful manipulation of patronage politics, Chea Sim was able to extend his power from the center into the provinces through the appointment of his clients to various important party and government positions (Gottesman, 2003: 105–106). Through this informal personal network, Chea Sim was able to wield enormous power, allowing him to overstep state institutions in carrying out his orders and protecting the interests of his clients (Gottesman, 2003: 217, 332–333).

Aware of the significance of patronage politics for political survival initially and for political domination eventually, Hun Sen by the middle of the 1980s began to build his own networks. By carefully avoiding confrontation with Chea Sim, Hun Sen played Chea Sim's game, cultivating his own network of loyalists in the provinces. By using his power inside the central government to maintain a secure space for the protection of provincial officials' interests and power bases, Hun Sen was able to co-opt many influential and at times violent figures. These networks became increasingly salient in the early 1990s because of intra-party rivalry within the CPP and inter-party rivalry between the CPP and the royalist National United Front for an Independent, Neutral, Peaceful and Cooperative Cambodia (FUNCINPEC). Efforts at consolidating networks fueled, Gottesman (2003: 211) points out, "a sprawling and heterogeneous network of ministries, agencies, and provincial and local administrations whose members adhered to the rules of patronage."

Hun Sen's political astuteness and oratorical talent placed him at the helm of the CPP during the peace negotiation process of the late 1980s and early 1990s. Hun Sen capitalized on this advantage to bolster his power within the CPP and thus the government at the further expense of Chea Sim's network. By the time of the 1993 elections, as Michael Vickery (1994: 114) points out, "If there was a split within the CPP, power within the party seems effectively to have passed from Chea Sim's group to that of Hun Sen." As Cambodia opened to the global political and economic system, Hun Sen gradually expanded his network to encompass not only key individuals in the security forces, but also business tycoons and intellectuals (Heder, 2005) and the CPP's powerful Central Committee. By the early 2000s, Hun Sen had become Cambodia's singular "strongman."

Given Hun Sen's domination over Cambodian politics, some analysts suggest that Cambodia is a personalist dictatorship.[3] Although Hun Sen wields decisive power on many issues, there are key signs suggesting that the current regime in Cambodia is not a personalist dictatorship. First, Hun Sen continues to work through the CPP structure in appointing senior government officials and adopting electoral strategies and mobilizing voters. Second, Hun Sen remains cautious in managing factions and frictions within his ruling party. The absence of concrete punitive actions against corruption and abuse of power by government officials following his strong public rhetoric against them suggests Hun Sen's absence of absolute power. Similar to other polities with entrenched patron-clientelism (Eisenstadt and Roniger, 1984), such lack of concrete punitive actions derives from the fact that Hun Sen's power rests on support of lesser patrons. In the meantime, these lesser patrons rely on him at the top of the pyramid. Such mutual reliance in turn leads Hun Sen to avoid the risk of alienating these lesser patrons. Consequently, Hun Sen shores up these lesser patrons' power and avoids the risk of alienating them by accommodating their requests, tolerating their behavior, and protecting their interests. Sorpong Peou (2001b: 59) cogently explains Cambodia's patronage-based structure:

> [T]he Prime Minister's political survival continues to depend on the goodwill of other CPP officials and military leaders who have also reaped the benefits from the CPP's political hegemony. Those who have benefited from Hun Sen's grip on power are those who have helped to keep him in power.

It should be noted that FUNCINPEC under the leadership of Prince Norodom Ranariddh also functioned through patronage. These conditions formed informal networks of entrenched patron-clientelism that affect state institutions, state capacity, and as a consequence undermine the quality of democracy. Under patron-clientelism, state coercive capacity is strong while other dimensions such as voice and accountability, government effectiveness, and regulatory quality are consistently weak (Kaufman and Kraay, 2016).

2.2 Patronage, Security Forces, and Coercion

In Cambodia, patron-clientelism is embedded in all state institutions, including the security forces. Consequently, although they are weak in terms of an absence of professionalism, they are strong in their ability to suppress the ruling party's political opponents, intimidate and threaten voters and protect

---

[3] For further discussion see Morgenbesser (2017).

networks of crony capitalism. In the first several years following the creation of a coalition government in 1993, the Cambodian military was fractious, with some elements aligning themselves behind FUNCINPEC while other supported the CPP. Following the 1997 coup, when forces loyal to then Second Prime Minister Hun Sen deposed then First Prime Minister Prince Norodom Ranariddh, the former was able to impose centralized control over the armed forces. However, the military would continue to operate under the covert rules of patronage and corruption. Securing loyalty through promotions has led to a bloated military security sector whose structure resembles a "reverse pyramid" (Far Eastern Economic Review, 1994).

Despite government efforts at military reform, factional politics and the CPP's goal of maintaining its political domination, this reverse pyramid structure lives on. It was reported in 2014 that the Royal Cambodian Armed Forces had over 2,200 generals of all ranks (some 1,500 more generals than in the entire U.S. military!) (Radio Free Asia, 2014). Heightened political tension following the CPP's crackdown on the opposition party and civil society groups in 2017 prompted Prime Minister Hun Sen to extend his patronage within the military by promoting an additional 1,250 officers to the rank of general raising the total number of generals to over 3,000 (Mech, 2017). As the military is structured based on patronage and personal loyalty, it is neither professional nor neutral. Research found that the military has been involved in a range of human rights abuses and other illegal activities such as logging and land grabbing (Global Witness, 2007).

The presence of suspicion and fear, both within the CPP and, in the 1990s between FUNCINPEC and the CPP, led Prime Minister Hun Sen to personalize key elements of the security forces. Soon after the 1993 elections, Hun Sen accused unspecified politicians of plotting to take revenge against him when they learned that the CPP would lose the elections. In his statement excerpted by SPK (1993), the official new agency of the State of Cambodia, Hun Sen said:

> Great numbers of fellow Cambodians have shown their pain on my behalf because even before the official announcement of the electoral result and complaints of the Cambodian People's Party [would be resolved] and a number of other political parties, there are people who not only demand to remove me [from power] but also attempt to bring me to trial. The act of revenge has begun like the saying, which states that "when water rises fish eats ants; when water recedes ants eat fish" (*pel teuk laoeng trey si sramaoch pel teuk haoc sramaoch si trey*). What crime did I commit which led me to face such injustice? … I have become the victim and this is a sign that revenge will occur in Cambodia in the future … If revenge could happen to me what will happen to my subordinates."

During the political maneuvering after the 1993 elections, the internal political struggle between the Hun Sen and Chea Sim networks over the premiership intensified. Chea Sim intended to replace Hun Sen with his protégé, Sar Kheng, a move that Hun Sen fiercely and successfully resisted (Far Eastern Economic Review, 1993a; 1993b). According to Hun Sen, elements within the CPP and FUNCINPEC attempted to remove him from power through different plots. Responding to a question by a journalist regarding who sought to arrest him in June 1993, Hun Sen stated:

> It was a person in the CPP, and this person also staged an abortive coup on July 2, 1994. General Sin Song, who has died. Another one, who is now a Senate member, Sin Sen. At the time they arrested me, Sin Sen was not present. I don't want to talk any more about this. Now I am like a cat people threw hot water on, so I don't let myself be frightened by cold water. Three times already. I will not allow the fourth.
>
> First, on June 2, 1993; second, on July 2 1994, and then July 5, 1997, when it was announced I had died . . .[4] (The Cambodia Daily, 2002).

Real fear and paranoia have prompted Hun Sen to build and maintain a well-equipped, well-funded and well-fed bodyguard unit numbering between 2,000 to 3,000 soldiers and a reserve unit known as Unit 70. The Bodyguard Unit (BHQ) is answerable only to Prime Minister Hun Sen. The BHQ has been implicated in attacks on opposition groups over the years. For instance, investigation by human rights groups and the US FBI implicated the BHQ in the grenade attacks that killed sixteen people and injured over a hundred Sam Rainsy Party supporters in 1997. That same year, too, the BHQ played a leading role in the violence that toppled Prince Norodom Ranariddh, then his co-Prime Minister, and ongoing harassment and suppression of opposition parties (Human Rights Watch, 2009). Following the 2013 elections, the BHQ were seen to intimidate Cambodia National Rescue Party (CNRP) through its exercises around the party's headquarters. Moreover, three of its members were involved in beating CNRP parliamentarians outside of the National Assembly Building in 2015. These three soldiers, after serving brief jail time, received promotions to the rank of colonel and general respectively (Meach and Turton, 2017).

Prime Minister Hun Sen has repeatedly stated that there are no other institutions or individuals who can control the armed forces other than himself. Consequently, his removal either by legitimate elections or other means would plunge Cambodia into civil war. Senior military officers openly declare

---

[4] The third was not a coup against him. Actually, it was initiated by him to oust then First Prime Minister Norodom Ranariddh, who was alleged to be allied with the Khmer Rouge to attack the capital.

their allegiance not to the state but to the CPP and Prime Minister Hun Sen. They have publicly threatened to crack down on any individuals or political parties who attempt to organize a "color revolution" against Hun Sen/CPP (Radio Free Asia, 2015). In the CPP's view, a color revolution is a movement demonstrating an alliance between civil society and an opposition party aided by the West to overthrow the government via mass protest. Arguably, Hun Sen's threats, the military's open support for Hun Sen, and past use of a military unit to crackdown on protesters, effectively silenced CNRP's supporters following the party's dissolution in 2017.

2.3 Oversight Institutions

Because of a justice system's unique capacity to level the playing field in the realm of economics, politics, society, and culture, it was hoped that a constitutionally enshrined independent justice system might enable Cambodia to deepen its democracy and to strengthen its institutions. Thus, the framers of the PPA ensured that Cambodia's new constitution guaranteed an independent judiciary. Article 128 of the Constitution specifies that the judicial body "shall be an independent power and shall guarantee and uphold impartiality and protect the rights and freedoms of the citizens." Article 130 stipulates that: "Judicial power shall not be granted to either the legislative or the executive branch."[5]

To safeguard the system of checks and balances, the government established complex judicial institutions to review, adjudicate, and enforce laws. The regular courts consist of three tiers – the courts of first instance, an Appeals Court, and the Supreme Court.[6] Situated atop this system is the Supreme Council of Magistracy (SCM) whose constitutional role (articles 132 and 133) is to assist the King to ensure the independence of the judiciary, and to recommend judges and prosecutors for royal appointment, dismissal and discipline. Although the Constitution empowers the monarch to oversee the judicial system, in reality he is just a figurehead. Moreover, the Constitution grants the Constitutional Council (CC) veto power to ensure the constitutionality of laws, rules, and regulations, and to resolve electoral disputes.

The discourse of judicial independence, effectiveness, and responsiveness enshrined in the 1993 constitution is novel to Cambodia. It was a shot in the dark. French colonial rule introduced a quasi-modern legal system in the late

---

[5] Constitution of the Kingdom of Cambodia, 1993. Available at: www.wipo.int/edocs/lexdocs/laws/en/kh/kh009en.pdf (Accessed October 3, 2018).

[6] The author's fieldwork suggests that the government under the Council for Legal and Judicial Reform has, since the early 2000s, drawn up a blue print for the creation of specialized courts.

nineteenth century, and it operated in Cambodia until 1975 when Cambodia fell under the radical regime of Democratic Kampuchea (DK). Right up to the rise of DK, there is no evidence that this judicial system ever acted as a check or balance against those in power. In fact, it was notoriously corrupt.[7]

The DK regime did not have even the "pretense of legality," (Vickery, 1986, 120) as it terminated the existing legal system by killing most members of Cambodian's legal profession, and destroying or converting to other uses legal resources such as schools, court buildings, books, and legal texts. Arrests, sentencing, and executions were made through arbitrary decisions of DK cadres acting in the name of *Angkar* ("the organization"), resulting in massive crimes against humanity, war crimes, and genocide.[8]

Thus, when the PRK came to power in 1979 following the fall of the DK regime, there was no legal system in place. The new regime therefore had to at least institute a pretense of legality. The PRK established a communist judicial system following Vietnamese and Soviet models. To address staff shortages, the PRK organized short-term training courses for would be judges and prosecutors (Donovan, 1993: 181–182). However, due to the regime's consideration of the legal system as an integral part of the regime's communist party apparatus, the training emphasized Marxist-Leninist doctrines over legal subjects and recruitment of prosecutors and judges was based on "good biography," meaning that they had correct political standing (Gottesman, 2003: 243–244).

Although the PRK slowly created a formal judicial system, party ideology subsumed legal procedures, resulting in frequent interference into the judicial process by government/party officials at both the central and provincial level. The party or powerful individuals determined the course of proceedings and the verdicts of trials. During a meeting at the council of Ministers in 1986 a former Minister of Justice complained: "Sentencing depends on the influence of persons offering an opinion, not on the law." (Gottesman, 2003: 254).

The above conditions have become path-dependent, impeding efforts at promoting rule of law and an independent judiciary in the post-international intervention era. Cambodia's current legal system began with a severe shortage in human resources. Initial shortages resulted in part from the execution of lawyers, judges, and legal scholars by the Khmer Rouge during its reign and the subsequent absence of a government policy for training new judges. However, the situation has improved since the early

---

[7] I thank Dr. David Chandler for this point.

[8] For details on the trials of former top Khmer Rouge leaders consult the Extraordinary Chambers in the Courts of Cambodia at www.eccc.gov.kh/en/node/39457.

2000s (Transparency International, 2007: 186). By 2017 an increasing number of Cambodian lawyers received formal legal training, but given a highly corrupt and entrenched patronage society few exhibit legal professionalism. Private Cambodian lawyers play the role of *nak rot kar* or "fixer/broker" (intermediary between litigants, prosecutors, and judges) rather than an "advocate of cases" (Khy, 2017; Un, 2009).

The highly politicized nature of Cambodian governance and the judicial system render it impossible for judges and prosecutors to maintain an independent stance. Everything comes down to politics, argues a prosecutor, because "The characteristics of politics determine the peculiarity of the court system" (J23, September 25, 2002).[9] As judges and prosecutors owe their careers to their parties or their patrons, they must frame their decisions within the context of, as one court official put it (over a decade ago, but it remains true today), "who offered them the seat" (J32, November 20, 2001). Consequently, in past rulings over political cases no evidence was needed, "advice" from the top was sufficient.

In recent years, the Cambodian government has adopted a more sophisticated use of the judiciary found in other electoral authoritarian regime such as Singapore and Malaysia (McCarthy and Un, 2017). Guillermo O'Donnell (2004: 40) calls these practices "rule by law" meaning that "For my friends, everything; for my enemies, the law." Although advice from the top is still needed for political cases and other cases involved individuals with wealth and political connections, the government provides the courts with broad laws to legitimize their rulings on political cases. Within this context, the CPP has passed and amended several key laws, such as the Defamation Law, the Anti-Corruption Law, the Law on Associations and Non-Governmental Organizations, and Laws on Political Parties and on the Election of Members of the National Assembly. The government, as discussion below, also uses the courts to suppress civil society organizations and opposition parties.

The SCM is designed to play a critical constitutional role in judicial oversight and review, serving as auxiliary to the King to ensure the independence of the judicial system. According to articles 133 and 134 of the Constitution, the SCM is responsible for recommending all judicial appointments, suspension, and disciplinary actions against judges and prosecutors, which are nominally executed by royal decrees. Like other judicial institutions in the country, many see the SCM as politically dependent, under the CPP influence, and

---

[9] This Element uses letters "D," "G," "J," and "N" to identify interviewees from the diplomatic corps and international bilateral institutions, government officials, members of the judicial branch, and members of civil society respectively. Not using interviewee names is in compliance with Northern Illinois University protection of human subjects regulations.

functionally weak (Lao, 1998). Moreover, like other state institutions, the SCM is embedded in the overarching system of patronage.[10] As a result, given the corrupt and erratic nature of the court system, legal actions by the SCM against corrupt practices and judicial misconduct have been rare and cosmetic. A prominent human rights defender states: "Punishments have occurred but they are inconsequential such as transferring to another province or city, or verbal warning" (N2, July 19, 2017).

In theory, the government's efforts in recent years at reforming the SMC could have lead to more professionalism within the judiciary. Key among these efforts was the passage of three major laws: the Law on the Organization and Functioning of the Supreme Council of Magistracy, the Law on the Statue of Judges and Prosecutors, and the Law on the Organization of the Courts. The National Assembly passed all three in 2014 while the opposition party was boycotting the legislature. These laws grant the Ministry of Justice broad power, however, including to chair the SMC, appoint the leadership of the SMC secretariat, manage the courts' budget, and appoint, promote, transfer, suspend, and remove judges and prosecutors. Consequently, given the Ministry of Justice's prominent role within the SMC, these laws do not necessarily lead to judicial independence.

The CC is another oversight institution that, according to the Constitution, has review power over the issue of constitutionality of already promulgated laws or decisions of state institutions and serve as the ultimate appellate body for political parties and citizens seek redress over violations of civil and political rights by the government. According to its website, "Citizens, party to legal proceedings, can raise the question of the unconstitutionality of the law or decision of state institutions such as Royal decrees, *prakas* (ministerial proclamation), and other administrative decisions" (the Constitutional Council of Cambodia). These constitutional stipulations theoretically force other institutions, particularly the legislature and the executive, to take the preferences of the CC and the public for that matter into account when forming and implementing policies. Furthermore, the CC serves as the last arbiter of complaints concerning electoral disputes.

Over the decade following its inception in 1998, the CC's legitimacy has remained in doubt, with criticisms coming particularly from the opposition parties and from at least one of its own former members. Responding to a question on the function of the CC, Son Soubert, a former member, said: "The Constitutional Council is tied up and bound. We cannot act on our own

---

[10] Author's field interviews with judges, prosecutors, clerks, and human rights workers over the course of more than a decade.

initiative, only when we receive a complaint. Even if a law is unconstitutional we cannot act. The Constitutional Council doesn't work" (The Phnom Penh Post Staff, 2007).[11] Therefore, over the past years, the principle of judicial review has not been fully applied. More directly detrimental to democratic process is the Council's inability to play the role of a fair, independent arbiter of electoral conflicts. Consequently, opposition parties see the Council "as a pawn of a political game" (Hughes and Real, 2000: 152). This perception is confirmed by the CC's ruling in favor of the CPP in electoral conflicts (Lewis and Kuch, 2013). In the end, opposition parties have resorted to street demonstrations and/or boycott of the National Assembly as the only viable venues to challenge the election results. The government has in turn responded to the opposition's strategies with violent use of force, threats, and co-optation. As the threat from the opposition became preeminent, the government resorted to banning the CNRP in 2017. Such actions further generated societal mistrust in the system and mistrust among political competitors, undermining any efforts at promoting democracy.

As far as legislative process is concerned, manipulation by the executive branch is the norm. Both the legislative and the executive branches can introduce legislation. However, due to the legislative branch's low capacity, and more critically its lack of independence, legislation normally originates from the government. The executive branch regularly controls the drafting process. Legislation submitted by the government to the National Assembly tends to arrive late and to be vague. These conditions provide the Council of Ministers great latitude in implementing legislation through enactment of sub-decrees. Consequently, contrary to their apparent aim of promoting good governance and transparency, in many instances, some new laws simply create new opportunities for rent seeking and arbitrary behavior for ministries and their officials through the issuance of *prakas* (Kato, 2000: 105). The developments surrounding classification of state land and land concessions discussed later in this section are exemplary reflections of the absence of judicial review and the occurrence of arbitrary decision making by the executive branch. These developments further reflect how the absence of inter-institutional accountability has helped to perpetuate Cambodia's patronage system and violate the rights and livelihoods of hundreds of thousands of families.

3 Patronage, Resource Mobilization, and Aid Dependency

Despite widespread patronage and rent seeking, given the country's location in an economically dynamic region and inflows of international aid, Cambodia's

---

[11] See also Lao (2006).

economy has grown at a substantial rate of around 7 percent per annum since the early 2000s.[12] Given Cambodia's economic transformation, the proportion of people working in agriculture has decreased from an average of 79 percent of the total workforce in the 1990s to 26.7 percent in 2017. Correspondingly, during this period the proportion of people employed in the service sector (including tourism) rose from 16.5 percent to 46.3 percent, while the proportion of employment in the industrial sector (including construction) increased from 4.5 percent in the 1990s to 27 percent in 2017. Construction and manufacturing have experienced the most rapid expansion. The garment industry – the core of the industrial sector – has become the backbone of the Cambodian economy, serving as the primary source of exports and industrial employment. By 2018, this sector contributed 80 percent of Cambodia's total recorded exports, provided well over 800,000 factory jobs (Spiess, 2018), and employed hundreds of thousands more indirectly.

Over the past decade, the number of out-of-country migrant workers also increased exponentially, with Thailand and South Korea as the top destinations. By 2018, the number of documented Cambodian migrant workers in Thailand exceeded one million with an estimated additional 30,000 undocumented ones (Meta, 2018); and documented workers in South Korea numbered around 53,000 by 2017 (Cheang, 2017). Inside Cambodia, workers' association with trade unions and other forms of socialization in the cities exposed them to progressive ideas as well as the extravagant life-style of city elites. Overseas Khmer workers came to admire development and competence of the governments of their host countries. Migrant workers' remittances have helped many cash-strapped families throughout the country. Furthermore, through their remittances, these workers have influence over their families' electoral choices which, in many cases, are in favor of the opposition party.

3.1 Corruption

In neo-patrimonial systems, corruption is widespread. Corruption is conceived not only in terms of engagement in procedural, substantive, or administrative behavior for private gain or to benefit family members or a close private clique, but also the illegal acquisition of resources to benefit an official's political party or to maintain a regime. The interlocking of neo-patronialism with electoral politics and a market economy has resulted in increased levels of crony capitalism and political corruption, as state actors and non-state actors collude

---

[12] Figures in this paragraph, unless otherwise stated, are drawn from World Bank data available at: https://data.worldbank.org/indicator (accessed August 18, 2018).

in parallel economies in which state officials – to use Rene Lemarchand's phrase (1988: 163) – act as "privileged partners in the management of economic exploitation."

Corruption is an inescapable daily reality of life in Cambodia wherein people are forced to bribe government officials in matters ranging from land registration to birth certificates, traffic citations, and taxation. The list is seemingly endless. Cambodians in all walks of life are aware of the magnitude of corruption in their country, believing that corruption has become the norm. The conventional understanding among the Cambodian public is that for a person given an opportunity to enrich himself through corruption not to take advantage of it would be not conscientious behavior but stupid or even crazy. For example, a survey conducted in 1998 by the Center for Social Development (1998:7), found that "84 percent of Cambodians believe that bribery is the normal way of doing business." Over a decade later, popular perception of corruption remains high, "82% of Cambodians believe that corruption is a problem in Cambodia" (PACT-Cambodia, 2010: p. 35). A 2016 Cambodia Enterprise Survey reports "almost 65% of Cambodian firms experienced at least one bribe request [when] dealing with access to utilities, permits, licenses and taxes" (World Bank, 2016).

Payment becomes a condition of employment in a pyramidal patron-client structure, as each tier purchases its positions from the one above it.[13] Moreover, under these conditions, while low ranking civil servants supplemented their meager incomes with petty corruption they impose on citizens and businesses, senior bureaucrats and party apparatchik enrich themselves through the issuance of monopolistic licenses for businesses or for natural resource extraction. It is the norm that officials at each echelon of government pass up part of their proceeds to their patrons on a regular basis, in an informal payment system known as "*sraom sambot chong khae*" or "the end of the month envelopes." As such, there is no incentive for patrons to punish their clients for "corruption" as long as the clients play by patronage rules. What Evan Gottesman wrote over a decade ago (2003: 335), remains true today and that is "as long as the money flows, officials act with impunity – engaging in theft, extortion or worse."

Consequently, government efforts to fight against corruption have been slow and largely cosmetic. Before the passage of the anti-corruption law in early 2010, foreign donors and civil society organizations argued that the absence of an anti-corruption law in Cambodia made anti-corruption efforts ineffective. However, since even before the passage of the anti-corruption law, Cambodia

---

[13] Author's conversations with government officials.

has had accountability institutions such as the National Audit Authority, the Ministry of National Assembly and Senate Relations and Inspection, and within-ministry Departments of Inspection that are in theory responsible for fighting corrupt practices. However, these institutions' inability to curb corruption is due to their inherent weaknesses, including a lack of capital and human resources, independence and transparency, and the presence of embedded patronage even within these units. Consequently, what Cambodia Development Resource Institute and Asian Development Bank (2000: 106) described continues to reflect the reality of Cambodia today: "most officials have been to varying degrees co-opted by the system. It is difficult for people with unclean hands to point a finger at others."

Under pressure from donors, the National Assembly passed an anti-corruption law in 2010 with a seemingly powerful enforcer – the Anti-Corruption Unit (ACU). The anti-corruption law requires senior government officials to declare their assets in a sealed envelope which only the ACU can access. The ACU will open the envelope of any official who is under investigation. Arguably such a requirement aims to extract political loyalty more than to curb corruption because most members of the ruling elites are thoroughly compromised by corruption. In the past few years, the ACU charged a few government officials, judges, prosecutors, and lower level members of the security forces with corruption. To some extent, the presence of the ACU has made government officials more cautious in engaging in bribery. As a senior official at a multi-lateral institution said, "they know someone is watching over their shoulders" (D 7, August 2, 2011). However, there has been no indication that rent-reeking at the higher echelons of the government has declined. Although, "petty corruption has declined, grand corruption and political corruption have not declined" (Preap Kol, August 2, 2017). Recent trends suggest that corruption in Cambodia is following the pattern of corruption in Indonesia under Soeharto. Corruption in critical sectors such as revenue collection, government procurement, licenses, and permits for natural resource extraction has been organized into a franchise system wherein franchisers (top government or party leaders) license franchisees (their clients) to collect rents.[14] The following discussion on revenue collection and the expropriation of natural resources illustrates the scale of corruption and crony capitalism and the adverse impact of these phenomena on the state's ability to mobilize resources.

---

[14] For discussion of corruption under Soeharto see McLeod (2000).

3.2 Revenue Collection

The Cambodian government's low level of revenue mobilization can be attributed to widespread patron-clientelism and corruption. The government, through public forums and policy papers, consistently acknowledges this problem. With pressure and assistance from Western donors, the Cambodian government began to implement public finance reforms in early 2000s (Hughes and Un, 2007). The government made some improvements in revenue collection; government tax collection increased from 9.6 percent of gross domestic product (GDP) in 2006 to 13.7 percent in 2013 (World Bank, 2018). However, corruption continued to be rampant and widespread within the public finance sector.

Following the 2013 elections, when the Cambodian People's Party (CPP) won a narrow majority in a controversial election allegedly marred with irregularities, the party realized that as the economy expanded and voters became more informed, they were increasing their demands for improved social services. At the same time, civil servants also demanded a salary increase. To respond to these demands, the government needed to further improve its revenue collection capacity. In 2013, Prime Minister Hun Sen therefore issued an ultimatum for the Customs Department to increase its revenue collection. Since then there have been significant reforms in public financial management. A senior official of a multilateral financial institution said: "Only within one year after the 2013 elections, the reforms in public finance amounted to the combined reforms of the previous five years" (D3, October 10, 2014). As a result, government revenue increased from 13.8 per cent in 2013 to 17.4 per cent in 2016 (World Bank, 2018). However, collusion between tax collectors and businesses, and leakages at the Ministry of Economy and Finance (MoEF) persist. This is unsurprising as these custom officers paid bribes to secure their positions and get rich with the purpose of staying rich. As top leadership demanded increased revenue collection, customs officers and businesses renegotiated tax payments. At the end of the day, businesses paid higher taxes than they previously did, but the new rate still did not truly reflect the scale of their businesses.[15] In return, tax collectors demanded higher "tea money" from businesses for assisting them to evade tax.

As well as businesses, government agencies also need to pay "tea money" to officials at MoEF in order to receive funding approval.[16] Typically, a government institution obtains only around 60 percent of its allocated

---

[15] Author's discussion with several business owners in Phnom Penh in 2015, 2016, and 2017.

[16] Author's discussion with a number of government officials from January–May 2015.

operational funds. These conditions, in combination with further leakages within each ministry, severely and adversely affect the function of government ministries and agencies and their ability to serve the public.[17] Further, government non-transparent procurement and contracts cause additional leakage.[18]

3.2.1 Natural Resource Expropriation

The intertwining relation between neo-patrimonialism and corruption unsurprisingly extends to the national resource sectors, particularly to forests and land. Due to ongoing civil war and weak central government before the formation of the post-UNTAC (United Nations Transitional Authority in Cambodia) government, logging was decentralized such that sub-national governments, provincial power brokers, and regional military leaders all benefitted. For a brief period, the post-UNTAC government attempted to centralize forest management but it then reversed course back to decentralization for two major reasons. The first was the need for the military's allegiance critical for the inter- and intra-party political struggles between and within FUNCINPEC (National United Front for an Independent, Neutral, Peaceful and Cooperative Cambodia) and the CPP. The second was the government's need for military support to fight against the remnants of the Khmer Rouge guerrilla movement. Under the period of re-decentralization, the army colluded with networks of business people and government officials to sell timber for personal gain and to raise funds to support themselves in the midst of low government budget (Le Billon, 2002: 570; World Bank, 2003a: 8).

The patronage-based expropriation of natural resources has deprived the government of much needed revenues. Speaking at a conference on corruption and its impact on national reconstruction held in 1995, the then Minister of Economy and Finance, Keat Chhun, estimated that through illegal logging, rubber exports, and fishing, the state was losing around US$100 million annually (Center for Social Development, 1998: 9). The losses increased over time. In 1997, Global Witness, an international environmental watchdog group, reported that revenues lost from the timber sector alone tallied US$309 million, amounting to 73 percent of that year's budget of US$419 million (Kyne, 1999).[19] Although this figure appears high, a conservative estimate by the World Bank confirms a remarkably high level of revenue lost from illegal logging. With reference to corruption, an internal World Bank report (2003a: 8) states:

---

[17] Author's conversation with government officials and staff at multilateral institutions 2013–2018.

[18] Author's field note, June–July 2017; June–July 2018.

[19] See also Global Witness (1998).

Over the last decade, forest revenues have seldom exceeded US $10 million per year and in 2001 were only US$7.7 million ... In contrast, in 1996 the World Bank estimated that forestry could sustainably generate as much as US$100 million in royalty revenues.

It should be noted that although the total peace Cambodia achieved, compounded by Prime Minister Hun Sen's consolidation of power, ended the once decentralized management of natural resources, it did not permit the government to achieve its stated objective of utilizing the country's natural resources for inclusive development. By the early 2000s, a number of changes had shifted crony-capitalist natural resource expropriation from logging toward land. First, years of rampant logging had exhausted Cambodia's forests. Second, Cambodia's deeper integration into regional and global economies created the potential for its comparative advantage in agricultural production. Domestic and foreign companies expressed interests in land acquisition. In response to rising demand for land, the government adopted a policy of Economic Land Concessions – long term lease of land to private companies – aimed at promoting employment and generating revenue. Given Cambodia's embedded crony-capitalism, the new government land concession policies opened opportunities for more centralized corrupt practices involving what a 2007 Global Witness report calls "kleptocratic elites,"[20] who colluded with each other to acquire large areas of land concessions. Devastatingly, these "kleptocratic elites" also exploited Cambodia's weak rule of law and patronage to continue to fell tropical forest trees beyond concessionary plantation boundaries.[21]

Cambodia's entrenched patronage order permitted exploitation of these land concession policies. The government granted companies permits in a non-transparent manner, exceeding the limit of 10,000 hectares per company specified by the 2002 land law (UNHCHR, 2007). For instance, Pheapimex Company, a major sponsor of the CPP, holds land concessions equivalent to 7.4 percent of the total land area in Cambodia (Global Witness, 2007, 10). Since the early 2000s, the Cambodian government has provided land concessions to foreign firms for agro-plantations especially (Global Witness, 2013). Leading foreign investors are Vietnamese and Chinese companies (May, 2014).

The combination of an absence of ownership rights, a corrupt judiciary, and patronage meant land concessions resulted in widespread land grabbing, depriving ethnic communities and farmers' access to agricultural land, and

---

[20] They include senior government officials, senior military officers, and business tycoons.

[21] This occurs, for instance, at the Tumring Rubber Plantation in Kampong Thom Province. See for example, Global Witness (2007); Cochrane (2007).

community forests with devastating effects on their livelihoods (Sloth, Khlok and Heov, 2005). Investigation by the Cambodian League for the Promotion and Defense of Human Rights (LICADO, 2014) place the number of people affected by land grabbing at over half a million between 2000 and 2014. With access to legal redress blocked, peasants often gathered outside the Royal Palace or the Prime Minister's residence – a testimony of an impassionate plea for help. As their plight was being ignored, victims of land grabs became impatient. In some areas affected communities organized protests and in most cases they were often met with violent government crackdowns. In response to domestic and international criticisms, and in efforts to improve the ruling party's image before the general elections scheduled for 2013, the Cambodian government launched a land-titling program in 2012. However, the results of the titling program have been mixed; in many cases it has been misused to legalize the kleptocratic elite capture of state land (Beban, So and Un, 2017).

Because of entrenched patronage, the government's objective of generating revenues from Economic Land Concessions for national development has not materialized. Non-transparent concessions have meant that much of the leasing fees do not enter state coffers and the concessionary plantations' ability to offer employment is extremely limited (Un and So, 2011: 299). Furthermore, entrenched patronage has impeded the government's ability to address landlessness problems, which have become more prevalent in rural Cambodia. The government claimed not to have adequate "free land" for redistribution under the Land for Social and Economic Development Project (2001), designed to provide social land concessions to the landless and "land poor" as a poverty reduction measure. Amidst its claims of shortage of arable land, there have been cases wherein the government reclassified "state public land," which is reserved for public domain into "state private land," which is eligible for transfer to private owners by executive fiat without any judicial review so that the latter could be awarded to politically well-connected business tycoons as concessions (Un and So, 2011: 296).

Today landlessness and small land holdings are the primary factors behind rural poverty (William, 1999; World Bank, 2006a), while considerable concentration of land ownership has become more prevalent due to governmental land concessions and land purchases. By the early 2000s, the situation was critical: while the bottom 40 percent of socio-economic strata owned 5.4 percent of the arable land, the top 20 percent owned 70 percent of the land, of which 64.4 percent was owned by the top 10 percent (Dapice, 2005: 15; World Bank, 2007: 5). As later discussion illustrates, crony-based land concessions become a salient political rallying point for the opposition party in the 2013 general elections.

In sum, the Cambodian state is captured by patronage networks; consequently, it has limited ability to mobilize resources for infrastructure development and public service provision. In the midst of the state's weak capacity, the CPP leaders have relied on the resources generated through patronage networks to consolidate and legitimize their rule. Under these conditions, as a CPP party official explained, "the state depends on the ruling party; the ruling party depends on individual party-cum state officials who in turn depend on rent seeking" as a mechanism for resource mobilization (G20 August 12, 2017). Through these patronage networks, CPP and government leaders have proclaimed themselves to be the benefactors, or *suboroschun* in Khmer, who aid the development of rural Cambodia via the "culture of sharing" (Hughes, 2006). The CPP and its leaders have dispensed their "own" resources to construct schools, roads, bridges, temples, and irrigation networks throughout the countryside (Pak and Craig, 2011; Un, 2005).

In many localities, the CPP even use these patronage handouts as a form of perverse accountability wherein the party hold voters accountable for their votes (Stokes, 2005) in the process of Cambodia's electoral authoritarianism. The CPP in its role as government also utilizes patronage-based resources to cultivate support from the armed forces. For example, in 2010 the government officially established patronage relationships between military units and private companies aimed at, in the words of the government's public statement, "sol[ving] the dire situation of the armed forces, police, military police and their families through a culture of sharing" (Bopha and Wallace, 2010).

3.3 Aid Dependency

Corruption and low levels of economic development mean that Cambodia has not been able to generate sufficient resources to address the country's dire need for infrastructure development and service provision. Because of a shortfall of resources, the Cambodian state has relied on financial assistance from Western donors and more recently the People's Republic of China. Such dependence, as subsequent sections discuss, has influenced the development of democracy in Cambodia. The international intervention of the early 1990s legitimized the Cambodian government, allowing it to have access to multi-lateral and bilateral economic assistance. Since the United Nations-sponsored elections in 1993, the international community – through Official Development Assistance (ODA) – has engaged in reconstructing the Cambodian state and economy.

The total amount of ODA between 1993 and 2015 was over US$12.5 billion (World Bank, 2017a). ODA constituted, on average, approximately 77 per cent of the annual Cambodian central government expenses from 2002 to 2015. Although the ratio of ODA to government budget has declined in recent years given the increasing size of the government budget, ODA still constituted approximately 30-40 percent of the government budget between 2013 and 2015 (World Bank, 2017b). Furthermore, Western governments also granted preferential trade status to Cambodia allowing the country to expand its export in agricultural produce and apparel.

The Hun Sen government has also increasingly relied on assistance from China. The watershed for a close Sino-Khmer tie began in 1997 when Prime Minister Hun Sen urgently needed a powerful non-Western ally to prop-up his government's international legitimacy following his internationally condemned violent ouster of his democratically elected senior coalition partner, Prince Norodom Ranariddh (Chanda, 2002). Under pressure from the United States to punish Prime Minister Hun Sen for this power grab, the United Nations Security Council voted to leave Cambodia's seat at the United Nations vacant while Western donors suspended their financial assistance to Cambodia. To offset the halt in international diplomatic and financial support for his cash-strapped and isolated government, Prime Minister Hun Sen wooed China through the prompt closure of Taiwan's trade office in Phnom Penh (Marks, 2000). Ever since, Sino-Cambodian relations have solidified.

On the diplomatic front, Cambodia and China have engaged in exchanges of visits of their top leaders. Noticeably, since 2000 all sitting Chinese presidents and Prime Ministers have visited Cambodia. Prime Minister Hun Sen has visited China more than ten times since 1998. Accompanying each of the visits was the signing of major comprehensive agreements between the two countries covering financial assistance, investment, trade, and military collaboration.

Moreover, Chinese development assistance to Cambodia not only dramatically increased but also diversified to include both bilateral and multilateral assistance. In 2007, as part of its expanding involvement in multilateral institutions, China's contribution to Cambodia through the Consultative Group (a donor coordination forum in Cambodia; since 2007 known as Cambodia Development Cooperation Forum) amounted to US$91.5 million out of the US$689 million total multilateral package to Cambodia (Lum and Vaughn, 2008). In 2016, China's overseas development assistance to Cambodia accounted for 36% of the total 732 million dollars of bilateral aid (Reuters, 2018b). In the past few years, China has also provided financial assistance to

Cambodian non-governmental organizations. According to AidData, the total amount of China's aid including grants and concessional loans and other assistance to Cambodia from 2000 to 2014 totaled nearly US$10 billion (Dreher et al., 2017).

By the early 2000s, China had already become Cambodia's "primary economic patron" (Lum and Vaughn, 2008). *The Economist* (2017) reported that, "Between 2011 and 2015 Chinese firms funneled nearly US$5bn in loans and investment to Cambodia, accounting for around 70% of the total industrial investment in the country." In 2017 alone, Chinese firms invested US$1.1 billion just in the coastal city of Sihanoukville (Ellis-Petersen, 2018). This dramatic increase made China by far the largest investor in Cambodia in the areas of critical natural resources, construction and hydropower plants, and agro-businesses. China's investment in Cambodia had the backing of the Chinese Communist Party and is facilitated by senior CPP leaders including Prime Minister Hun Sen.

China also has strong bilateral trade with Cambodia. China has waived tariffs for over 400 products from Cambodia, over 90 percent of which are agricultural goods and raw materials (Kynge, Haddou, and Peel, 2016). Bilateral trade between the two countries shot from US$933 million in 2007 to US$2.83 billion in 2013, and reached US$5 billion by 2017, though the balance of trade heavily favors China (Parameswaran, 2018).

The governments of both China and Cambodia claim that China's aid "has no strings attached." To the contrary, China has geo-political and economic interests in Cambodia. China promotes a like-minded government friendly to China; secures priority access to investment, particularly natural resources and; promotes pro-China foreign policy, especially in the South China Sea region (Sothirak Pou, 23 July 2018). China and several Association of Southeast Asian Nations (ASEAN) members have overlapping claims in the South China Sea where the major contention is between China, Vietnam, and the Philippines. Cambodia has twice demonstrated its loyalty to China in the latter's territorial conflicts with Southeast Asian claimants through blocking ASEAN consensus on issuing critical statements pertaining to China's aggressive posture in the South China Sea (Lewis, 2012; Mogato, Marina, and Blanchard, 2016).

Western donors to a great extent have been able to link their development assistance and their preferential trade access directly to Cambodia's willingness to maintain democracy and to protect human rights. However, the Cambodian government's commitment to promoting democracy and human rights have been lukewarm at best. Instead of allowing liberal democracy to develop, the Cambodian government has been determined to maintain electoral authoritarianism. Western donors appear to accept that as a fait accompli for the following reasons. First and foremost, donors' interests dovetail with their belief in Hun Sen's ability to maintain peace, stability, and thus economic growth. Second, Western donors lack unity due to their divergent geo-political and economic interests. France and Japan have strong investment in Cambodia. In addition, Japan also intends to balance China's influence in Cambodia. The resulting consequence is that donors are not consistent, unified, or forceful in pressuring the government for change (D1, June 10, 2003). The former United States Ambassador to Cambodia, Charles Ray, concurs that lack of unity, consistency, and forcefulness among donors is "one of the biggest problems" his embassy faces in dealing with the government. He went on to say that "If I do this the French would be mad. If I do that the Japanese would be mad. But the Cambodian government used it as an excuse not to carry out reform."[22] As the remaining sections demonstrate, because of the complexities of democracy promotion, Western donors remain engaged with the Hun Sen regime so long as the latter allows some semblance of democracy to exist. In the meantime, the CPP agreed to maintain such political order as long as there were no credible challenges to its power. However, when a credible challenge to its power emerged, the CPP resorted to authoritarian measures and used its close relations with China to counter-leverage Western pressure.

4 Parties, Elections, and Civil Society under Electoral Authoritarianism

Through the United Nations' intervention in 1993, the international community planned to establish liberal democracy in Cambodia. However, the Cambodian ruling party was determined to maintain its domination over Cambodian politics. Prime Minister Hun Sen proclaimed during a meeting in 1989 in anticipation of an internationally imposed democratization that: "If there is a political solution and if [opposition politicians] come [onto the political scene], there should be a mutual give and take. They repay us by recognizing us as the central leader. We repay them by recognizing them as a legal party" (Gottesman, 2003: 306). This section examines the domination of the Cambodian People's Party (CPP) through the maintenance of electoral authoritarianism, and the absence initially of any credible counter-movement to the CPP. More specifically, this section analyzes first, the varying strategies the CPP has employed to maintain electoral authoritarianism; second, the

---

[22] Charles Ray, Remarks by US Ambassador to Cambodia at the Cambodian Association of Illinois, Chicago, May 2007.

weaknesses and disunity of the opposition parties; and third, challenges preventing Cambodian civil society organizations from serving as a countervailing force to the CPP.

4.1 Shift From Coercion To Patronage

Cambodia's electoral regime has its origins in the United Nations' intervention in 1993. Due to the Khmer Rouge boycott of the Paris Peace Agreement (PPA), the United Nations Transitional Authority in Cambodia (UNTAC) was unable to fully control all of Cambodia administratively; however, it was able to create a competitive electoral environment with free information, and intense political campaigning by multiple political parties. The conditions permitted Cambodian electorate in 1993 to display notably rational behavior. As David Chandler writes, "A majority of Cambodians had voted against an armed, incumbent government. Unlike most Cambodian voters in the past, they had courageously rejected the status quo" (Chandler, 2008: 288). The royalist National United Front for an Independent, Neutral, Peaceful and Cooperative Cambodia (FUNCINPEC) party captured 45 percent of the total vote, while the CPP received 38 percent. However, the CPP's dominant position going into the election would determine the trajectory of the externally imposed democratization.

Following its stunning electoral defeat, the CPP was quickly able, given its military strength and control over a deep state, to shoulder its way back within the democratic framework into state control, forcing FUNCINPEC into a subordinate position within a coalition government. Between 1993 and 1997, the CPP and FUNCINPEC in general and Hun Sen and Prince Norodom Ranariddh in particular, were locked in a test of strength that eventually exploded in a two-day bloody conflict in July 1997 that decimated FUNCINPEC (Peou, 2001a). Because Cambodia represented a showcase for international post-Cold War peace and democracy building, the international community – especially the United States – was determined not to let Cambodia be judged as a failed project. It therefore pressured the Hun Sen government to agree to hold the first post-UNTAC election on schedule in 1998 (Peou, 1998).

In Cambodia, during the 1990s, like in many other developing countries, "the city becomes the continuing center of opposition to the political system" (Huntington, 1996: 433). Urban voters are more sophisticated and inclined to support parties with specific policies aimed at addressing pressing issues affecting their daily lives, such as corruption, cronyism, unfair treatment of small businesses, and political freedom. Additionally, Phnom

Penh – Cambodia's mega city – enjoyed a relatively high level of press freedom, diverse economic activities, a better educated public, and multiple sources of protection made possible by the presence of international organizations and Western embassies. The urban electorate has generally been able to resist the CPP-dominated state's attempts at coercion and co-optation (Hughes, 2003).

The urban combination of pluralist voices, a relatively sophisticated electorate, and open political space placed the CPP at a relative electoral disadvantage vis-à-vis the opposition political parties. Under these conditions, the ruling party has focused on cultivating the support of rural residents. The opening strategy included the limiting of a rural stage for open opposition political activities and the systematic surveillance of rural voters. The CPP carefully limited the opening up of the hinterland to the political opposition, finally doing so only on its own terms and only when it was confident in its ability to attract rural supporters (Un and Ledgerwood, 2003).

The process of political decentralization which began in 2002, through direct elections of commune councils – representing clusters of villages – exemplified the CPP's controlled opening of rural space. The CPP had held a monopoly over local authorities ever since the defeat of the Khmer Rouge in 1979. After the 1993 elections, FUNCINPEC pushed for commune elections, but was stymied by CPP objections. Consequently, the commune chiefs appointed during the PRK and SoC periods continued to dominate local level government throughout the 1990s and early 2000s. These authorities offered the CPP a base for a national chain of patron-client networks that ensured the party's accumulation of power and its extension across the entire country. The commune chiefs also served as the mechanism for the CPP's system of surveillance and intimidation of villagers and opposition party activists (Un, 2011; Hughes, 2003). Among the surveillance tactics used were the organization of villagers into groups of ten persons who were shepherded to the polls under the watchful eyes of CPP-trusted local activists and included the collection of thumbprints and forced pledges of allegiance from voters. These tactics were designed to generate a climate of fear that, as Caroline Hughes (2003: 72) suggests, "was used explicitly to prevent villagers not only from voting and campaigning for other parties, but also from receiving information about other parties."

Despite the fact that intimidation, surveillance, and violence continued right up to just before the 1998 elections, the result of the elections reflected the ineffectiveness of CPP's foul tactics (Bjornlund, 2001). The combined vote totals that FUNCINPEC and the Sam Rainsy Party (SRP) received – 46 percent of the total votes – was higher than the 42 percent the CPP obtained. However, because the allocation of seats is based on the "highest average" (d'Hondt) formula, which favors larger parties, the CPP received the plurality of seats in the National Assembly.[23] The election results indicated that a sizeable number of voters still believed in FUNCINPEC and were willing to give the party a second chance, while a significant number of people, particularly urban dwellers, entrusted the SRP with their votes. As such, it was the division of the opposition parties rather than intimidation and violence alone that contributed to the victory of the CPP (Un, 2005; Hughes, 2013).

The 1998 election results demonstrated that CPP coercion, intimidation, and violence did not constitute a foundation for permanent strength. Given widespread international outcry and domestic resistance, the CPP shifted tactics to seek external and internal legitimacy linked to acceptable electoral outcomes. With this in mind, the CPP pivoted toward material inducements to win the "hearts and minds" of rural voters and to undercut competition from opposition parties. This was the beginning of the development of mass patronage electoral politics through which the CPP organized central government officials in their role as party officials, state institutions, and national and provincial businesses into machine politics known as "party working groups" (PWG). These political machines, which are linked hierarchically to the CPP, permeate, supersede, and operate parallel to state institutions in channeling resources and personnel to local communities.

The CPP modeled PWGs after an old People's Republic of Kampuchea (PRK)/CPP blueprint but with new messages and inducements that reflected Cambodia's neo-patrimonial state and the growing phenomenon of crony capitalism. The old PRK/CPP model of the 1980s was known as *choh moulthan* (going down to the base). In that period, the ruling party sent groups of party cadres to the countryside to disseminate party propaganda in an effort to raise people's revolutionary spirit to fight the return of the Khmer Rouge and to build socialism. Members of PWGs then disseminated the "Three Nos and One Report" (*bey min mouy reaykar*) throughout the PRK-controlled territories. The "Three Nos" were: don't believe in the enemy's propaganda; don't hide the enemy; don't participate in the enemy's activities; the "One Report" recorded all activities raised against the revolution and the "people's interests." During the period leading up to the 1993 elections, the CPP reconstituted the "working groups," whose members visited local communities warning people not to vote for the opposition parties, which the CPP portrayed as nothing but the Khmer Rouge in disguise (Frieson, 1996).

---

[23] For discussion of Cambodia's electoral system please see Croissant (2016).

The current PWG resources derive from three sources. The first is contributions from government officials. It is a CPP rule that across government ministries and agencies a portion of funds generated through rent seeking has to be reserved for electoral campaigns. This is known as "black box money" (Un, 2005). Beginning in 2017, due to the unpopularity of those required contributions among middle and low level government officials, the CPP began to make contributions from these groups voluntary. However, promotion and other privileges for government officials remain tied to the level of contribution to the party.[24] The second source of contributions is business tycoons. It is common to see CPP ministers who head PWGs having links to business tycoons whose companies are under the minister's jurisdiction. The third source comes from the CPP's headquarters (Pak and Craig, 2011).

In many communities, villagers see the CPP working groups as able agents who make up for local government's shortcomings in promoting local development and in assisting local communities in times of crisis. Decentralization introduced in 2002 had two objectives: to institute democracy at the local level, and to promote economic development through local participation. Decentralization's second objective of alleviating poverty through local participatory development remains largely unrealized due to local councils' lack of resources and the absence of autonomy (Rusten et al., 2004; Eng and Ear, 2016). In the midst of the challenges facing local government, the PWGs' development funds reached local communities regularly, quickly, and in some areas at almost double the amounts provided by the state (Pak and Craig, 2011). Therefore, I argued in 2008, "[d]espite persistent poverty, the majority of Cambodians, particularly those [in] rural areas, now see the state under CPP control as a 'predatory state' that has been transformed into a welcome 'service state'" (Un, 2008a: 2). But the appeal of such a strategy lasted only for a limited time period; the reasons for which will become clear below.

Additionally, patronage politics has been part of Prime Minister Hun Sen's imagining himself as the embodiment of Cambodia, as the nation's benefactor (*saboroschun*) dedicated to the "culture of sharing" (Norén-Nilsson, 2016a; Hughes 2006). As the paramount patron of Cambodia's neo-patrimonial system, Prime Minister Hun Sen has sponsored such large and very visible projects as schools, roads, bridges, and inter-district irrigation networks. Although a significant portion of this funding came from foreign aid, the rest originated from the Prime Minister's resources personally mobilized

---

[24] Author's field-notes, June–July, 2017.

from his political and economic clients. Pro-government and state television footage often shows Prime Minister Hun Sen answering requests made by representatives of villagers who have gathered to listen to his marathon speeches. Upon receiving requests, followed by nods of assurance from the business tycoons accompanying him, the Prime Minister would then proclaim, "presented as requested" (*choun tam samnaum por*) (Un, 2005). A pro-Hun Sen letter sent to a local newspaper illustrates the centrality of the Prime Minister's imagination of himself as the embodiment of Cambodia and its development:

> Even though Samdech Prime Minister Hun Sen was not born in the Royal family, he leads the country better than other kings. It can be said that in Khmer history, none of the Cambodians kings has been able to do things like Samdech Prime Minister Hun Sen.
> Where are there any Khmer leaders including Cambodian kings in all generations, who have built more schools than Samdech Hun Sen? Samdech Prime Minister Hun Sen is the only person who has built more than 2,000 schools (Roum Rik, 2003).

In addition, PWGs also offered small gifts during the election cycles which contain hidden threats. One of the CPP's tactics employed until after the 2013 elections was the classification of voters into categories that would be eligible for patronage handouts: "white" for CPP's supporters, "black" for opposition parties' supporters, and "grey" for ambiguous voters. These gifts and PWG funded infrastructure project influenced many voters' decisions in the 2003, 2008, and 2012 local elections. As Caroline Hughes (2003:76) argues, the risk of exclusion was high if voters refused the gifts, because to do so was not "merely unprofitable but physically threatening." Given rural poverty, CPP's perceived surveillance capabilities, and the relative geographical immobility of rural voters, at a time when everyone knew everyone else in the village, it was difficult for rural voters to receive gifts from the CPP and then renege.

My own conversations with villagers before the 2003 elections revealed that they voted for the CPP because of the party's ability to offer them tangible resources. A villager in Kompong Cham province, for example, said a couple weeks before the 2003 election that many people in her village were considering voting for the CPP because the party promised to build a dinner hall for monks at the village temple (author's conversation with villagers, Kampong Cham July 02, 2003). Within patronage politics and with asymmetrical power among political parties and a weak state, the dominant party can also employ perverse accountability. In answer to my query in Kampong Speu as to why the main road running through their village had not been fixed, while roads in other places had been, villagers said that it was because local people had voted for FUNCINPEC in 1998. However, they added, "Many people are thinking of voting for the CPP this time in order to get the road fixed" (authors' interview with villagers in Kampong Speu, July 18, 2003). In the 2003 Asia Foundation survey, only 13 percent of likely voters stated that they would vote according to the urging of local leaders, while close to two-thirds "cited the delivery of material resources by the party as one of their main reasons for choosing a party" (Asia Foundation, 2003: 49). The International Republican Institute's (IRI) multiple-year public opinion surveys likewise have shown that among Cambodians who believed that their country is "headed in the right direction," the majority listed the development of infrastructure such as schools, roads, bridges, and irrigation networks as the reason for this conclusion.[25]

4.2 Opposition Disunity

Like in other dominant party authoritarian regimes, the CPP's electoral domination is also associated with its relative strength vis-à-vis opposition parties. The CPP's strength derives from its control over the state apparatus and resources and its internal unity. It should also be noted that despite the presence of factions and friction within the CPP, the party has maintained a united front in its dealings with political rivals. As in other cases of electoral authoritarianism, the fundamental factor underlying the CPP's unity is its members' shared notion of enduring hardship – in their case, during their fight against the Khmer Rouge in the late 1970s and the subsequent civil war and international isolation of the 1980s and early 1990s. As Khieu Kanhariddh, a Central Committee Member of the CPP and a close ally of Hun Sen, stated "the CPP never lets its members die" (Khieu Khannariddh, June 16, 2005). Furthermore, party unity allows members of the neo-patrimonial order to continue to benefit from the spoils of the regime. This unity allows the CPP to preserve and expand its power and therefore the perpetuation of electoral authoritarianism.

Given the significance of party unity, the ruling CPP also employed divide and rule tactics against its opponents. The fate of the Khmer Nation Party (KNP) was an outcome of such CPP tactics. Because of his criticism of corruption within the government and the lack of progress in political and economic reform, Sam Rainsy was expelled from the National Assembly and

---

[25] International Republican Institutions, Survey of Cambodian Public Opinion, 2007, 2008, 2009, 2010, 2011, 2012, 2013 and 2014. Online www.iri.org/country/cambodia (accessed September 12, 2018).

fired from his post as the Minister of Economy and Finance in 1995. Following this episode and despite numerous threats, Sam Rainsy founded a new political party, the KNP. He then intensified his criticism of the government and its leaders, particularly Hun Sen and Prince Ranariddh. The new party faced intimidation and confinement of its activities to urban areas. Even though the government eventually allowed the KNP to establish offices in rural areas, the authorities continued to harass its members. In 1997, the KNP splintered into two factions. The general belief was that the CPP engineered the split through its support of renegades within the party. A pro-CPP splinter faction claimed leadership and ownership of the party name and logo from the Sam Rainsy group, sparking a protracted legal battle in a pro-CPP courtroom. With no prospect of a favor settlement in sight, Sam Rainsy eventually opted to create a new political party, the SRP, in 1997. Similar splits occurred within the two other major opposition political parties – FUNCINPEC and the Buddhist Liberal Democratic Party (BLDP) – around the same period.

Employing his new SRP as a mechanism for popular mobilization, Rainsy continued to push for a more expansive forum for public debate and deliberation through urban protests that sought to expose government failings and corruption. His confrontational stance resulted in several attempts on his life. The nearest miss occurred in March 1997, when four grenades were tossed at him while he was leading a protest demanding judicial reform in front of the national assembly. The explosions killed 16 people and wounded 100, with Rainsy barely escaping death (Barber and Chaumau, 1997). Those involved in this atrocity have never been found. In the meantime, a number of SRP's grassroots activists and journalists thought to have links with the KNP and subsequently the SRP were assassinated (Shawcross 1994). The government also used its controlled judiciary to harass Sam Rainsy and SRP members.

FUNCINPEC, the first credible challenger to the CPP, became politically irrelevant by 2005 for three main reasons. The 1993 election saw the majority of Cambodians give FUNCINPEC a mandate to undertake the challenge of rebuilding Cambodia. In the midst of CPP resistance, this was a daunting task for FUNCINPEC and its leadership. The CPP's deep state made every efforts to undermine FUNCINPEC including a coup against then First Prime Minister Ranariddh in 1997. The coup decimated FUNCINPEC's military forces, effectively ending any meaningful bargaining power the party had. Following the coup, FUNCINPEC adopted a non-confrontational stance toward the CPP. Equally detrimental to FUNCINPEC is Prince Ranariddh's poor leadership. According to a former senior FUNCINPEC leader, rather than challenging the CPP, FUNCINPEC adopted a policy based on the principle of four Cs: coalition, cooperation, and competition without confrontation. Although the principle of the four Cs brought about political stability, they did not position FUNCINPEC as an alternative to the CPP for Cambodians who were dissatisfied with CPP rule (Un and Ledgerwood, 2003: 115).

When faced with challenges, instead of assuming a leadership role and laying out a vision for the nation, Prince Ranariddh appeared to be "happy with the trappings of power and unwilling to fight for the substance" (Shawcross, 1994: 40–44, 93). Although this remark was made in 1993, it continues to effectively characterize Prince Ranariddh's leadership until now (Norén-Nilsson, 2016a). His lackluster leadership generated divisions within FUNCINPEC and led to defections and expulsions of key party members. The ejection of Sam Rainsy from FUNCINPEC was a severe loss to the party. Instead of backing Sam Rainsy in his efforts to expose the Hun Sen dominated government's weaknesses, Prince Ranariddh colluded with Hun Sen to force Sam Rainsy from his post as Minister of Economy and Finance in 1994. A year later, Prince Ranarridh orchestrated the expulsion of Sam Rainsy from FUNCINPEC. As explained above, Sam Rainsy then created the KNP, then subsequently SRP (Un, 2008b; Norén-Nilsson, 2016a).

Another critical development affecting FUNCINPEC was the departure of Kem Sokha from the party in 2002 to form the Cambodian Center for Human Rights (CCHR) and subsequently the Human Rights Party (HRP) in 2007. Furthermore, FUNCINPEC failed to formulate an agenda that reflected the ongoing changes in Cambodia. Rather, it relied on its royal roots to mobilize supporters. Its campaign platform was based on royal achievements during "the golden era of Sihanouk rule" in the '50s and '60s, a message that no longer had much relevance for Cambodia's young demographic (Norén-Nilsson, 2016a).

Opposition parties had not only faced internal divisions, they also failed to form sustained inter-party collaboration until shortly before the 2013 elections, when Kem Sokha's HRP and Sam Rainsy's namesake SRP merged to form the Cambodian National Rescue Party (CNRP). Previously, inter-party alliances within the opposition camp were short-lived and their main objective had been to extract political concessions from the CPP, not to create a long-term unified opposition to the CPP's domination. For example, following the disputed 2003 elections, FUNCINPEC and SRP formed the Alliance of Democrats. It organized protests against electoral irregularities and boycotted the National Assembly. Prince Norodom Ranariddh of FUNCINPEC defected from this alliance, as he had in the past, to enter into a coalition government with Hun Sen, then joined Prime Minister Hun Sen in harassing Sam Rainsy with politically motivated defamation charges (McCarthy and Un, 2017).

4.3 State–Society Relations

Cambodia's electoral authoritarianism can be partly attributed to the fundamentally imbalanced relationship between the state and society at the time of the introduction of democracy to the country. Historically the Cambodian state was strong in terms of its capability to wield violence over society in ways that perpetuated the political and ideological interests of the elites while the society was weak, unorganized, and disengaged. These conditions worsened during the era of the Khmer Rouge social revolution, the ensuing civil war, and communist rule, resulting in the complete suppression of civil society (Chandler, 1998), the stratum of autonomous voluntary associational life between state and family (White, 1994: 379).

It was the arrival of UNTAC in 1992 that permitted the development in Cambodia of a national public sphere for political action and the formation of civil society organizations (CSOs) (Hughes, 2001). Through financial and political support from Western donors and transnational networks of nongovernmental organizations (NGOs), Cambodian CSOs, mainly NGOs, began to grow, forming the backbone of Cambodia's civil society. Indeed, until very recently the terms 'NGO' and 'civil society' were used synonymously in Cambodia. Available data in 2012 estimated the number of registered Cambodian NGOs numbered around 4,378 in 2012; however, only 1,315 were operational (Cooperation Committee for Cambodia, 2012).

Cambodian NGOs emerged under unfavorable conditions. The most challenging obstacle for NGOs is the government's hostile position toward them. For the government, there are "good NGOs" and "bad NGOs." The former are those that work to advance people's material needs for which the government can claim credit. "Bad" NGOs are human rights and democracy NGOs whose works constitute nothing positive from the government's perspective, but serve only to undermine it. For example, Prime Minister Hun Sen has often publicly ridiculed human rights and democracy NGOs – a position which was best captured in a 2002 interview:

> Many NGOs are working right at the target areas of poverty, for which they deserve our encouragement and respect. They have been living and working in the rural areas. But it seems some NGOs do not attach themselves to poverty reduction. I feel regret for the money given by some countries to such NGOs, which spend most of their time in the city and in hotels for seminars. You see them every day. They put on neckties and stay in air-conditioned rooms and act like a fourth branch of the government (*The Cambodia Daily*, 2002).

Prime Minister Hun Sen's negative views derive from his fear of NGOs' growth into a countervailing force to the CPP's domination, and from his ideological beliefs. In spite of the country's official proclamation of adherence to liberal democracy in 1993, Cambodian leaders never accepted this principle. Prime Minister Hun Sen rejected Western democracy while adhering to "popular democracy" – a conception that stresses rights to material well-being, social order and peace (Norén-Nilsson, 2016a: 128). Furthermore, the government suspected collusion among Western governments and international NGOs and Cambodian NGOs to undermine the government and to stir social and political instability. The government argues that human rights and democracy NGOs exist in order to ridicule the government for financial gain. For example, Prime Minister Hun Sen in 2008 stated that "Cambodia has been heaven for NGOs for too long … The NGOs are out of control … they insult the government just to ensure their financial survival" (Bessant, 2014).

Furthermore, the CPP-dominated government joined the ranks of many electoral authoritarian regimes such as Turkey, Russia, and Egypt in consistently questioning the neutrality of human rights and democracy NGOs, believing that they have, as a director of one NGO puts it, "some kind of political backing" (N3, January 15, 2003). Consequently, according to news reports and field interviews, the government labels advocacy Cambodian NGOs negatively as "secessionists," "agents of opposition parties," "supporters of perpetrators," and "obstructers of government development work" (N6, July 4, 2017).[26]

First, among the reasons for this fear and suspicion is that many leaders of human rights and democracy NGOs are overseas Khmers or former political prisoners who are strongly anti-authoritarian. Second, some of the issues for which these NGOs advocate such as the rule of law, anti-corruption, accountability, judicial reform, protection of human rights, and protection of natural resources, are also part of the opposition agenda. Third, these NGOs receive funding from foreign countries and international NGOs that are interested in promoting democracy and respect for human rights in Cambodia.

The government's negative stance towards advocacy NGOs meant it restricted their activities. To work in rural areas, especially during election periods, NGOs need to request permission from various levels of the government to conduct activities in rural areas. As one NGO worker complained during a Government–NGO Forum in 2015: "Even meeting under a tree

---

[26] See also, Naren and Seiff (2012).

requires permission from the authorities."[27] Despite its negative perception toward human rights and democracy NGOs, the Cambodian government continues to allow these NGOs to operate for two key reasons. The first is the leverage placed upon the Cambodian government by the international community through the conditions attached to its annual overseas development assistance to and trade preferences for Cambodia. Second, the CPP had been able to win consecutive elections without resorting to extensive repression of CSOs. Such electoral victories stem, as discussed above, from disunity within the opposition camp and the government's continued success in utilizing its patronage politics and control over the electoral process and institutions.

Another challenge for Cambodian NGOs is finances. Due critically to Cambodia's low level of development, and partly to the country's absence of a culture of philanthropy, domestic sources of funding are non-existent. Consequently, Cambodian NGOs need to rely exclusively on international financial support. As a result, Cambodian NGOs, some analysts argue, lack autonomy from their donors, conditions that have forced Cambodian NGOs to devote much of their resources toward fulfilling donor's priorities and agendas rather than focusing on resolving more pressing local and national issues. Furthermore, as donors' agendas for funding shifted, Cambodian NGOs' also needed to shift their activities (the Cooperation Committee for Cambodia, 2010; Hughes 2009a). Cambodian NGOs' exclusive reliance on foreign funding will continue into the foreseeable future given the absence of domestically generated resources. The consensus gathered through field interviews with representative of Cambodian CSOs in 2017 was that if donors terminated funding, most Cambodian CSOs would fold. It is indisputable that international donors have influence over Cambodian NGOs' agendas; however, these agendas, to a great extent, remain relevant to the Cambodian specific local and national issues such as gender equality, welfare, HIV prevention, education, governance, human rights, and democracy and anti-corruption. It is through NGOs' promotion of those issues that broad awareness of citizen's rights and other expectations of government activities and services deepen.

Cambodian NGOs also face difficulty in recruiting members. The absence of membership for most NGOs is the product of several factors, including the fact that Cambodian NGOs did not emerge out of, to use Salamon's terms, "spontaneous grass-roots energies" (Salamon, 1994: 112). Rather, they were the product of a top-down development involving a small number of people

---

[27] Author's field-notes, February 17, 2015.

who capitalized on the opportunities of a newly, but narrowly, opened political space and the availability of foreign funding. Also, Cambodian NGOs came into existence and grew in a society where people are generally disinclined towards, and lack a tradition of, forming associations. In the 1960s, the anthropologist May Ebihara (2018: 80) observed:

> A striking feature of Khmer village life is the lack of indigenous, traditional, organizational associations, clubs, factions, or other groups that are formed on non-kinship principles.

Although there are cooperative, reciprocal work teams formed for the purpose of labor exchange during the cultivating season or for construction projects, these teams are formed on an ad hoc and temporary basis.

As the aforementioned discussion shows, due to government surveillance and limited access to rural areas, NGOs, for a number of years following the UN intervention, faced difficulty in mobilizing people. Despite these challenges a few key democracy and human rights NGOs were able to create networks of informants. For instance, the Cambodian Human Rights and Development Association (ADHOC) has a few thousand activists who devote their time and effort, and bravely risk their lives to help ADHOC identify and monitor human rights abuses throughout the country. The Cambodian League for the Promotion and Defense of Human Rights (LICADO) also claims to have grassroots informants in about ten provinces, though their number is small and they are not organized into a network (N14, 08 January 2003; N7, September 5, 2018). The Committee for Free and Fair Elections in Cambodia (COMFREL) also has several thousand volunteers who help the organization to monitor elections.

Through international linkages and dedication, advocacy NGOs have been able to file reports documenting cases of human rights abuses, incidents of land grabbing, and illegal logging. These NGOs, though with limited success, have lobbied the government to undertake reforms in those areas. As a result, Cambodian NGOs have also been able to adapt, localize, and disseminate liberal ideas such as human rights, democracy, transparency, and accountability, which were absent in Cambodia's past political and social discourses (Ledgerwood and Un, 2003). Over time, public awareness of these discourses has taken root in Cambodia particularly among its youth (BBC World Service Trust, 2010). Doubts remained over Cambodian NGOs' ability to promote bottom-up demand for democracy due primarily to their lack of grassroots social mobilization for political change (Un, 2006). But these doubts began, to some extent, to lift by the early 2000s, as there were signs of NGOs forming networks to promote democracy.

Starting somewhere around 2003–2005, Cambodian civil society underwent remarkable transformation (N6, July 4, 2017). Civil society was no longer synonymous with NGOs; it had community-based organizations (CBOs) as new members. This expansion was made possible by three critical conditions; the first was the availability of local space for political participation associated with the government's policy of decentralization. After initial fierce resistance, in 2002 the ruling CPP agreed to local elections to select councils for communes – clusters of villages and urban neighborhoods. This process of political decentralization gradually paved the way for participatory political pluralism at the local level (Eng, 2014). Decentralization emphasizes local delivery of services ranging from education to healthcare to resource management. Because the government lacked capacity and resources to address local needs, it permitted local participation. These developments contributed to the dramatic growth of CBOs. By 2013, the estimated number of CBOs reached 25,000 (Ou and Kim, 2013). The combined existence of NGOs and CBOs filled in the former vacuum between state and society at the local level (Ojendal, 2013).

The second factor is people's increased awareness of their political rights accompanying the effects of intensified resource expropriation by networks of crony-capitalists on local communities and the declining appeal of CPP's patronage politics. The next section will further elaborate on this issue. The third factor is changes in donors' and NGO strategies. Cambodian NGOs' awareness of the significance of grass-roots movements has increased over time resulting from regional spill-over effects. Cambodian NGOs have sent their representatives to countries in the region such as the Philippines and Thailand to learn about social activism and grass-roots mobilization (N40, July 18, 2017; N6, July 4, 2017). Cambodian NGOs also learned about social activism from regional gatherings of NGOs which occurred in conjunction with Association of Southeast Asian Nations (ASEAN) annual gatherings, when NGOs shared their experiences and framed their strategies on how to promote democracy and human rights.

International donors and Cambodian NGOs began to see, as political scientist Steve Heder observes, the potential for "progressive social movement" associated with CBOs which "were class-based and mass based" (Heder, July 26, 2017). As a result, Cambodian NGOs and international donors shifted their collaborative emphasis from training projects on human rights to projects that promoted active citizenship through grassroots empowerment (Ou and Kim, 2013: 5–6).

Through years of engagement in rural development and training, NGOs have gained legitimacy among Cambodians. A recent survey revealed that NGO workers are the second most trusted people besides extended family members (Cambodia Development Resource Institute, 2018). The combined effects of increased popular political and rights awareness, shifting international donors' and Cambodian NGOs' strategies, as one prominent Cambodian social scientist notes, permitted NGOs "[to get to] the base and then push for change from the bottom up" (N40, July 18, 2017). In doing so, NGOs engaged in a number of critical activities; in areas without CBOs, Cambodian NGOs helped to create them. In areas already populated with CBOs, Cambodian NGOs helped to strengthen them in critical ways. Cambodian NGOs came to serve as inter-mediaries between donors and CBOs by channeling donors' funding to CBOs. This role is important because members of CBOs included farmers who have limited or no knowledge of English or the necessary accounting skills to file reports required by donors. NGOs provided legal counseling and training to CBOs, and they assisted CBOs to form networks. NGOs organized these networks physically if possible and virtually when necessary. For example, with the help of NGOs, communities that were affected by logging formed networks such as the Prey Lang Network which spanned multiple provinces to patrol protected forests to guard against illegal logging and demand the govern-ment take action against illegal loggers to preserve community forests. The Prey Lang Network has approximately 200,000 members spreading across multiple provinces (Verkoren and Ngin, 2017).

Manipulation of the electoral process is a common feature of an electoral authoritarian regime like Cambodia. Some Cambodian NGOs such as COMFREL through its bravery and professionalism have been able to expose the Cambodian government's electoral manipulation. During the national elec-tion cycle in 2013, COMFREL documented irregularities with voter lists including the deletion of names of voters (COMFREL, 2013). Such documen-tation gave legitimacy to the CNRP's post-election protests resulting in the reform of the National Election Committee.

Furthermore, through social media platforms, NGOs introduced Western symbols to CBOs so that the latter could employ them to draw international attention to their struggles. One example was NGOs' dissemination of an "Avatar" character from the movie of that name through YouTube and Facebook to community forest networks who then used it "as a symbol of land rights struggle" (N6, July 4, 2017). NGOs have also helped to coordinate meetings among CBOs and government agencies and representatives of poli-tical parties, and to provide logistics such as food and water during protests by CBOs (N6, 4 July 2017).

Another component of civil society is trade unions. The expansion of industry, particularly the garment sector, created fertile ground for unionization as the sector is linked to international markets, access to which requires good labor practices. For instance, in 1996 it was the Most Favored Nations status from the United States that linked the right to unionization in Cambodia to the latter's preferential access to the United States' market (Lang, 1996). In 2001, the European Union granted Cambodia preferential trade status under its "Everthing But Arms" scheme on the condition that the government respect human rights, workers' rights, and democracy (Clean Clothes Campaign, 2015). Realizing the potential of workers as a political group, Sam Rainsy helped to organize Cambodia's first trade unions, the Free Trade Union of Workers of the Kingdom of Cambodia, in 1996. Around the same time, the government also sponsored its own unions. By 2015, the total number of trade unions reached 3,000 (Rollet and Baliga, 2015). In broad terms, there are three groups of unions in Cambodia. The first group consists of unions that are politically, ideologically and/or financially supported by the government, thus labeled pro-government. The second group appears linked to opposition parties; however, it is unclear whether these unions actually obtain financial support from opposition parties. The third constitutes unions that are independent from political parties and receive support from international organizations (Nuon and Serrano 2010). These conditions mean that many trade unions' finances and ability to withstand the hostility of employers are contingent on support from the state and/or international organizations (Arnold 2017).

The primary concerns of all trade unions are wage increases and improved working conditions for workers; however, they adopt different approaches. While pro-government unions tend to engage in lobbying and compromise-seeking on wages and working conditions, pro-opposition and independent unions tend to engage in strikes to achieve their objectives (Hughes, 2007; Ford and Gillan, 2017). There are no horizontal linkages between trade unions and NGOs, as the latter consider the former political entities. NGOs are concerned that the government would see any affiliation between the two as political, which might risk government suppression.[28] Although pro-opposition and,possibly independent trade unions have offered political support to opposition groups, they have not posed critical challenges to the ruling party. Through its use of violence, intimidation, and infiltration into the labor union movement, the government has been able to keep trade unions under control.

This section has argued that the ruling CPP is skeptical of democracy; however, due to donors' demands to see some semblance of democracy in

---

[28] This information is based on my conversations with NGO leaders over the past few years.

Cambodia, the CPP has tempered its electoral authoritarianism with a certain degree of electoral competition and civil liberties. Nonetheless, the CPP used intimidation and material inducement, divide and rule tactics, and a politicized judiciary to ensure its domination. These strategies in combination with a weak civil society and a divided opposition, permitted the CPP to retain its political control without excessive political repression. However, the CPP could only flirt with such tempered electoral authoritarianism for a limited period of time. Economic growth accompanied by socio-economic transformation has generated broad political awareness among the Cambodian public. Along the way, opposition groups became united, serving as catalysts rallying a counter-movement against CPP domination. Facing these challenges the CPP has returned Cambodia to a more hegemonic variant of electoral authoritarianism, a move made possible, as detailed below, by its own strengths and increasing support from China.

5 The Rise of a Counter-movement to Electoral Authoritarianism

The Cambodian People's Party (CPP)'s overwhelming victories in the 2008 national and 2012 local elections lead some scholars to conclude that Cambodia had reached a state of hegemonic electoral authoritarianism – a condition wherein the same political party regularly secures the super majority of votes in any particular election (Diamond, 2002). Levitsky and Way (2010) characterized Cambodia's regime as "stable authoritarianism" wherein the CPP's ability to mobilize state resources for its patronage politics and capacity to manipulate state institutions to distort the electoral playing field that made any meaningful electoral challenge to the CPP impossible. Subsequent political developments show that such a conclusion was premature given the subsequent shift to more competitive electoral authoritarianism. The gap between the dominant party and the second party in number of seats they received declined drastically between 2008 and 2013 elections. In 2008 elections, while the CPP controlled 90 National Assembly seats, the runner up party, the Sam Rainsy Party (SRP), occupied only 26 seats. In contrast, in 2013 elections, while the CPP captured 68 seats, the opposition Cambodia National Rescue Party (CNRP) won 58 seats. This section analyzes factors accounting for the rise of the opposition to electoral competitiveness.

5.1 Economic Growth, Social Media, And Demographic Change

Key issues, which are associated with economic development, have helped foster opposition politics. First, Cambodia's economic growth of around

7 percent per annum since 2000 has facilitated dramatically increased access to information beyond traditional state-controlled and affiliated media – particularly a shift from radio to social media like Facebook. Confident of its strong electoral performance beginning with the 2003 and 2008 national elections, the CPP relaxed its control over radio broadcasting. Although the government continued to deny opposition parties' broadcasting licenses, it allowed independent radio stations such as Radio Free Asia, Voice of America, Independent Women's Radio, Voice of Democracy, and Beehive Radio to operate. The government also allowed provincial stations to relay broadcastings of those stations, making critical news on Cambodia's pressing issues such as deforestation, land grabbing, corruption, and poor service delivery, available to broad segments of the Cambodian population for the first time. As a result, Cambodians became increasingly aware of their rights while simultaneously seeing the effects of collusion between the state and big businesses on their livelihoods.

Concurrently, Cambodia's economic growth spurred growth in information/communication technology. The creation of Khmer Unicode around 2008 and the proliferation of smart-phones enabled a dramatic increase in the number of internet users. Websites, blogs, and social networks in Khmer proliferated (Phong, Srun and Sola, 2016: 1). The percentage of Cambodians who used the Internet to access news recently surpassed the number who watched TV and listened to radio, making Internet and Facebook especially, by 2016 "Cambodia's most important source of information about Cambodia" (Phong et al., 2016: 24). The number of people using Facebook in particular increased from 16 percent in 2013 to 23 percent in 2014, to 34 percent in 2015, and to 48 percent in 2016. A large portion of Facebook users (35 percent) stated that obtaining information is their priority for having a Facebook account (Phong et al., 2016: 17). Although the proportion of Cambodian Facebook users hovered around 48 percent in 2016 (Phong et al., 2016), Cambodians, especially those in the countryside, share Facebook feeds, suggesting that news spreads quickly, further fueling the already prevalent sharing of political news by word of mouth. Increased access to information raised popular awareness of crony-capitalism and social injustice. The emergence of social media networks in Khmer fostered wider "imagined communities," wherein issues that were once local in nature have become national, spawning a broad movement for political change.

The second factor contributing to the rise of counter-movement to electoral authoritarianism is demographic change. Since the turn of the century, Cambodia has experienced a youth bulge. In Cambodia in 2013, 3.5 million out of 9 million registered voters were aged between 18 and

30 (Ponniah, 2013). 1.5 million out of these 3.5 million registered youth had just reached voting age in time for the 2013 elections (Hughes, 2013). The youth have become increasingly politically active due to their geographical mobility in search of employment and their access to social media. More importantly, not only do the majority of these youth harbor discontent toward the status quo, but they are also in a position to influence their families' political views. Media reports and existing research reveal that social media have had significant influence over youth political activism. A 2014 study of 105 young Cambodian Facebook users revealed that 56.2 percent of the respondents showed a great deal of political interest, 39.1 percent displayed some political interest, and 4.8 percent exhibited little political interest (Thun, 2014). No respondent showed a total lack of political interest.

Additionally, these youths were not deterred by CPP's threats that if it lost the election, civil war could once again erupt. A CPP media campaign in 2017 that appeared to be directed toward Cambodian youth who might contemplate a "color revolution" made reference to the destruction, death, and prolonged civil war caused by the weakening of strongmen in other countries. The video portrayed the regret shown by a young man who presumably started the Syrian color revolution. The documentary film then asked the rhetorical question of whether Cambodian youth would want that to happen in their country (Press OCM, 2017). But the CPP's threats of war have been unlikely to register among Cambodian young voters who have no memory of the civil war and Khmer Rouge atrocities. In reference to Cambodian youth's lack of concern about war and their support for the CNRP, a long term former CPP commune chief stated: "Young people do not understand what war is like. It is a difficult situation for the country."[29]

Youth political activism, which greatly benefits the CNRP, is also associated with high rates of rural to urban migration and out of country migration in search of employment and other opportunities. Both pull factors – an exciting city life and employment opportunities – and push factors – rural poverty and lack of access to agricultural land caused by land atomization, land grabbing, or families' loss of land due to illnesses – have played critical roles in rural to urban and out of country migration. This migration has left villages across the country quiet. These migrant workers, owing to remittances they send to their families, have influence over their families' political views. For instance,

---

[29] Interview with author, Kandal Province, July 21, 2017.

a leading Cambodian social scientist states: "In places where there are more young people working in the cities or foreign countries, there are more supporters for CNRP" (N40, 18 July 2017).

Another factor contributing to the rise in counter-movement to electoral authoritarianism is people's changing attitudes toward the CPP's coercion and patronage. Years of civil war and the Khmer Rouge genocide traumatized Cambodians. However, as peace and memory of the Khmer Rouge atrocities and civil wars faded away, the CPP's projection of itself as the guarantor of peace and benefactor of rural development – within the context of rising expectations for social justice and responsive and accountable government – was much less appealing. Cambodian farmers still tend to be cautious, but many have become more tactically astute: while they might still express outward support for the CPP, many want change. Historically, when the party offered them gifts in exchange for a promise to vote for the CPP, they took the gifts and promised support. However, on election day in 2013, many then cast their ballots against the ruling party (Un, 2013b). This occurred because, as a 2014 Asia Foundation surveyed found, "virtually all Cambodians [98 percent] think that it was okay to accept money from a political party but to vote for the party they like" (Everett and Meisburger, 2014: 46). A shocking revelation by a member of a party working group (PWG) in Kandal Province tells it all: "I had 1200 villagers on my list under the 'White' (loyal) category; but only 300 voted for the CPP" (G 12, August 01, 2013).

As the discussion above on Cambodian civil society illustrates, during the 2000s, increased linkages between international non-governmental organizations (NGOs), donors, Cambodian NGOs, and community-based organizations (CBOs), in the context of social and economic injustice, generated heightened political activism at the local level. As a leader of an advocacy CNGO states: "Some CBOs are strong and active in advocacy because they are standing with water up to their nose; they have to struggle because they are losing their livelihood" (N39, 18 June 2013). Such activism took different forms ranging from public protests, to demanding government action to resolving issues of land grabbing and logging, to participating in the government land-titling program. The presence of active CBOs and their collaboration with Cambodian NGOs has contributed to more active participation of citizens, for example, in the land-titling program, which has helped ensure in some cases transparency and thus favorable outcomes for farmers (Beban et al., 2017).

The presence of CBOs and their networks, as the leader of a Cambodian NGO active in building networks of CBOs states, "offered [disaffected] people a platform to speak in one voice. They formed a constituency" (N39, July 4, 2017). She explained that because CBOs, NGOs, and opposition parties engaged in efforts to address such similar issues as lack of government responsiveness, corruption, and land grabbing, the growth in the number and activities of CBOs within the context of decentralization helped opposition parties to penetrate Cambodia's hinterland access long denied to them by the CPP's political intimidation, violence, and cultivated fear within rural communities. Later these conditions presented fertile recruitment ground for the opposition CNRP.

Increased political activism by unions is another contributing factor in the rise in counter-movement to electoral authoritarianism. Pro-opposition and independent unions became more vocal by the early 2000s in demanding wage increases. In the months leading up to the general elections in 2013, unions raised their wage demands to $160 per month. While the government argued such an increase would hurt the garment sector's competitiveness, the CNRP contended that such salary raise would not have any adverse effect on the industry if the government could curb bribes its officials demanded from the sector. As such, garment workers' concerns became politicized and central to both the populist campaign platform of the CNRP in the run up to the July 2013 elections and to subsequent protests from August 2013 to January 2014 over perceived electoral irregularities (Arnold, 2017). The CNRP attempted to mobilize on two fronts, one led by workers and the other by the general public, to put pressure on the CPP after the 2013 elections.

5.2 Opposition Unity

The above social, economic, and demographic changes were necessary but not sufficient conditions for a counter movement to meaningfully challenge the CPP's domination within the context of electoral authoritarianism. Any substantive challenge required the presence of a unified opposition to channel political discontent associated with increasing socio-economic injustice and people's rising expectations into an oppositional electoral force. With the exception of the 2008 election, the CPP has never won by a wide margin. Its strength has been based, in no small part, on the divisions within the opposition camp. The 2013 merger of the two major opposition parties, the Human Rights Party (HRP) and the SRP to form the CNRP, was important for a number of reasons including offering the Cambodian National Rescue Party (CNRP) a unified rural and urban base.

Table 5.1 Vote, Share, and Number of Seats for General Elections, 1993–2013

Political Party	1993		1998		2003		2008		2013		2018	
	Vote Share	Seats	Vote Share	Seats	Vote Share	Seats	Vote Share	Seats	Vote Share	Seats	Vote Share	Seats
CPP	38.2	51	41.4	64	47.35	73	58.11	90	48.83	68	76.85	125
FUNCINPEC	45.5	58	31.7	43	20.75	26	5.05	2	3.66	0	5.89	0
BLDP	3.8	10	N/A	N/A	N/A	N/A	N/A	N/A	N/A	N/A	N/A	N/A
MOULINAKA	1.4	1	N/A	N/A	N/A	N/A	N/A	N/A	N/A	N/A	N/A	N/A
SRP	N/A	N/A	14.3	15	21.87	24	21.93	26	N/A	N/A	N/A	N/A
HRP	N/A	N/A	N/A	N/A	N/A	N/A	6.62	3	N/A	N/A	N/A	N/A
CNRP	N/A	N/A	N/A	N/A	N/A	N/A	N/A	N/A	44.46	55	banned	N/A
Norodom Ranariddh	N/A	N/A	N/A	N/A	N/A	N/A	5.62	2	N/A	N/A	N/A	N/A

Source: Nohlen, Grotz, and Hartmann (2001); Hideyuki (2003); COMFREL (2013, 2017); National Election Committee (2018).

The HRP was built from the bottom up out of Kem Sokha's role as director of Cambodian Center for Human Rights (CCHR) in the earlier 2000s. During these years, with assistance from US-funded NGOs, Kem Sokha launched a radio program, the Voice of Democracy, and organized local forums on human rights and democracy throughout Cambodia. The Voice of Democracy and village meetings offered Kem Sokha a platform to discuss Cambodia's pressing social, political, and economic problems. Because of the Voice of Democracy broadcasts, village meetings, and other protest activities, Kem Sokha's popularity began to rise, making him the target of a government crackdown. He was arrested in 2005 on charges of defamation related to the sensitive issue of accusing Prime Minister Hun Sen of ceding Cambodian land to the Vietnamese (Working Group for an ASEAN Human Rights Mechanism, 2007). This arrest further raised Kem Sokha's public visibility, particularly among some segments of the urban population.

HRP's rural base complemented the SRP's urban base; the latter's strength came from its success in mobilizing disaffected groups – small merchants, workers, victims of land grabbing – into protest movements in the late 1990s and early 2000s. Sam Rainsy's success at popular political activation earned him the nickname of "the CEO of demonstrations." Using these urban-based movements, the SRP gradually expanded its activities into rural Cambodia despite strong CPP restrictions (Un, 2008b). Additionally, the merger between HRP and SRP united their respective overseas Khmer supporters, who increased their financial support to the CNRP.[30] This overseas Khmer support for the CNRP arose from their dissatisfaction with corruption, widespread poverty, and the presence of Vietnamese immigrants in Cambodia. For many overseas Khmers, Cambodia's persistent problems, such as poverty and limited democracy, originate with the Vietnamese, whom they see as continuing to control the CPP with the ultimate alleged intention of annexing Cambodia. As a result, they contributed substantial amounts of money to the CNRP, which allowed the party to expand its campaign activities (Soksan Hing, 20 June 2014).

Another contribution to the rise of counter-movement to electoral author-itarianism was the CNRP's effective campaigning. The CPP's major campaign themes were peace and stability, celebrating its role in liberating the country from the Khmer Rouge, and its commitment to further strengthening existing government policies that focus on infrastructure development and promotion of overall economic growth. The CPP's campaign ignored the negative

---

[30] This view is consistent with the author's personal conversations with overseas Khmers in the United States.

developments associated with such growth. Since the early 2000s, Cambodia had experienced sustained economic growth; however, as detailed above, amidst this growth there existed high levels of social injustice, corruption, inequality, cronyism, and incidents of land grabbing. These are issues that concern large segments of the Cambodian public in general and youth in particular. CNRP's clear, practical, and appealing campaign slogans reflected these concerns (Un, 2013b).

The opposition party also effectively capitalized on Cambodians' animosity toward Vietnam, linked to long historical roots as well as the more recent Vietnamese occupation of Cambodia in the 1980s. The CNRP promised immigration reform to curb what it called an uncontrolled influx of illegal Vietnamese into Cambodia and defense of Cambodian territory. Such an anti-Vietnamese campaign is appealing to some segments of the Cambodian public.[31] Crucially in the 2013 elections, the opposition was also able to successfully link the issue of Vietnamese domination of Cambodia to incidents of land grabbing. As the previous section shows, the last decade following Cambodia's integration into regional and global economies saw increasing foreign acquisition of land. In the few years leading to the elections in 2013, Vietnamese companies controlled the largest areas granted to foreign entities through land economic concession. The CNRP through social media and other platforms successfully linked popular fears over immigration from Vietnam to growing concerns that the government was selling the country's rich land, in the form of economic concessions, to Vietnamese companies. That campaign allowed the CNRP to turn discrete reports of expropriation of farmers' land into a much broader case against the wholesale exploitation of Cambodia's natural resources by an ill-intentioned neighbor (Un, 2015).

The rise of a counter-movement, including a single broad-based opposition party, discussed in this section made the 2013 elections the most competitive since the United Nations sponsored elections in 1993. As in other post-United Nations Transitional Authority in Cambodia (UNTAC) elections, civil society organizations, and opposition parties alleged irregularities. The official results of the 2013 national elections – notwithstanding allegations of irregularities – showed that the CNRP cut the CPP's super majority in the National Assembly from 90 seats to 68. Ensuing spontaneous protests sent an unequivocally clear signal to the CPP of the desire for

---

[31] According to the US Central Intelligence Agency, Vietnamese living and working in Cambodia account for 5 percent of the country's total population (15.4 million), which is equal to approximately 770,000 ethnic Vietnamese people (Central Intelligence Agency n.d.). Vietnamese constitute the second largest ethnic group in Cambodia after the Khmer.

leadership change among many Cambodians. Utilizing its 2013 electoral momentum, the CNRP was able through mass protests and boycott of the National Assembly to force the CPP to agree to reform the National Election Committee (NEC) making it more independent and transparent. These conditions, as the next section shows, set the stage for the CPP's decision to abandon the tempered electoral authoritarianism.

6 The Return to Authoritarianism

The political momentum the Cambodia National Rescue Party (CNRP) gained forced the Cambodian People's Party (CPP) to re-evaluate its options as to whether it would continue to flirt with reasonably fair elections or return Cambodia to authoritarianism. The CPP chose the latter. The following section examines four related factors: CPP's attempt at policy and strategy reform and its limited success in the local elections in 2017; CPP's lack of confidence in the minimally revised patronage system to lead it to victory in the 2018 elections; CPP's decision to return to authoritarianism as a preventative measure; and the role of China's engagement as an enabling factor for the CPP to withstand Western pressure.

6.1 Old Habits Die Hard

As in other electoral authoritarian regimes, the CPP initially upgraded its legitimacy by improving state services and patronage handouts, while also tightening its autocratic measures against its opponents. Although political patronage remains central to CPP operations, the party changed tactics. After the general elections in 2013 and in anticipation of the 2017 commune elections and the 2018 general elections, the CPP broadened its inclusive distribution policy, giving gifts not only to CPP supporters, but to every rural family at critical times such as childbirth, funerals and weddings, and generally to those in need.

As people's standards of living improve, and popular expectation rise, however, the value of basic patronage-based gifts in kind or in cash declines (Norén-Nilsson, 2016b). In lieu of CPP's petty gifts, voters want programmatic services from their government. A survey by the National Committee for Sub-national Democratic Development (2014) found that people's perceptions of local councils reflected people's dissatisfaction over the councils' inability or unwillingness to address their needs. One might wonder why the CPP even wastes its resources on patronage. First, according to some party apparatchiks, the fundamental problem for the CPP is that old habits die hard.[32] Second, given the inertia of state bureaucracy to

---

[32] Author's field-notes, 2018.

reform, the CPP believed that inclusive patronage might help to improve its popularity. After its drastic decline in popular support in 2013, the CPP had increased the national budget for social sectors such as healthcare and education. The CPP also co-opted the CNRP's campaign agenda, most crucially by advocating for salary increases for government employees, factory workers, and members of the security forces. The CPP further announced plans to increase government revenues and government funding for social services such as healthcare and education.

For the CPP, the effectiveness of its carrot and stick strategies to bolster the party's popular appeal remained unclear after the 2017 local level elections.[33] Many voters saw the CPP's 2013–2017 reform initiatives as too little too late. With a reformed National Election Committee (NEC), the CNRP was able to shrink the CPP's near monopoly over local councils. In 2012, the CPP won control of 97 percent of the total councils (1,592 of the 1,633 councils available), leaving Sam Rainsy Party (SRP) and Human Rights Party (HRP) in distant second and third places respectively (Un, 2013a). In the 2017 local elections, the CPP was able to hold on to 1,163 councils while the CNRP captured 482. More importantly, the total combined vote share won by the opposition camp increased from 32 percent in 2012 to 46 percent in 2017 (COMFREL, 2017). Unlike previous elections, the 2013 general and 2017 local elections showed that the CPP's level of support had fallen both in the urban and rural areas. These trends suggested that the opposition had finally penetrated rural areas that had been CPP strongholds.

The inability of old parties like National United Front for an Independent, Neutral, Peaceful and Cooperative Cambodia (FUNCINPEC) and new political parties like the Grassroots Democratic Party to capture any meaningful popular support in the 2017 local elections showed that Cambodia had effectively become a two-party system of CPP and CNRP, and future elections would be a direct one-on-one face-off. The outcome of the general elections in 2018 could have been a toss-up if the elections had been held under an impartial and professional NEC. Indeed, rumors and speculation abounded among informants in the months leading to the 2018 elections that a CPP's survey of how people would vote in the 2018 elections revealed that the majority of Cambodian voters wanted to replace the CPP with the CNRP.

Actually, the CPP began to lay the ground for the return to authoritarianism in 2015. In that year, the government started to impose stricter control over civil

---

[33] Local elections scheduled between national elections serve as a referendum on the ruling party's popularity.

society organizations (CSOs). In 2015, the CPP-controlled legislature finally passed the long floated restrictive Laws on Associations and Non-government Organizations (LANGO). The opposition party boycotted the vote. This law is widely believed to affect the constitutional right to freedom of association for non-governmental organizations (NGOs). Of critical concern for them is a requirement for the compulsory registration of all NGOs which states that "The Ministry of Interior may deny the request for registration of an association or non-governmental organization whose purpose and goal is found to endanger the security, stability and public order or jeopardize the national security, national unity, cultures, tradition, and good custom[s] of the Cambodian national society" (LANGO). This vague provision could provide for the selective denial of registration applications. In addition, there is a reporting requirement stipulated in article 25, chapter 5 of LANGO, requiring organizations to submit annual activity and financial reports, as well as to document donations received.

The government's position is that such requirements do not add additional work for NGOs nor affect their operations since NGOs are already required by their donors to submit their activity and financial reports (G20, June 27, 2017). Arguably, this provision has potentially negative effects on NGOs whose work focuses on sensitive issues like human rights violations, human trafficking, and legal aid that requires confidentiality (International Center for Non-Profit Law, 2018). Moreover, LANGO stipulates that "Domestic organizations, foreign non-governmental organizations, or foreign associations shall maintain their neutrality towards political parties in the Kingdom of Cambodia" (LANGO). This provision again is vague. In general, Cambodian NGOs perform roles dealing with politically sensitive issues such as promotion and protection of human rights and democracy, exposing rampant exploitation of natural resources by networks of crony-capitalists and protecting local communities from these forces. Therefore, their actions are intrinsically political. Furthermore, since opposition parties also campaign on similar issues to those on which NGOs focus, the government could easily accuse NGOs of having opposition leaning biases. LANGO's vague wording, compounded by politicized courts, allows the government broad latitude in interpreting the law. The government can deem many activities by NGOs as "political, inciting protest, inciting uprising, and defaming [the government]" (N6, July 4, 2017).

To pre-empt a potential electoral fallout, the CPP used its control over the National Assembly to change election and political party laws and then deploy the politically dependent courts to engineer convictions against opposition party leaders aimed at eliminating genuine political pluralism. The CPP amended the Law on Political Parties and the Law on Election of Members of the National Assembly to grant the courts' greater power to dissolve any political party found to violate the laws, to prohibit a convict from serving as leader of a political party, and create the mechanisms for redistributing of the seats of a dissolved political party (Meas and Handley, 2017). With the façade of rule of law framed, the CPP began to dismantle the opposition party, to further restrict civil liberties, and reconstitute surveillance and intimidation in rural areas.

The government's first action was to arrest Kem Sokha in September 2017 on charge of "treason" for collaboration with the United States to overthrow the Cambodian government. The government's second action was to have the Supreme Court dissolve the CNRP in November 2017, and to distribute its seats in the National Assembly and commune councils to other parties which won votes in the 2013 elections, and to ban 118 of its members from engaging in political activities for five years (Holmes, 2017).

Despite international protests and threat of economic sanctions, the CPP proceeded with the organization of the elections in 2018 without the participation of the CNRP. Twenty political parties participated in the elections. Due to their lack of popularity, grass-roots organizations, or clear policy agendas, none of them could pose any challenge to the CPP. Four small political parties – FUNCINPEC, the Grassroots Democracy Party, and the League for Democracy Party, and the Khmer Wisdom Party – have some degree of organizational structure at the sub-national level and therefore received some votes. Furthermore, most the 20 political parties are independent in name only but do not take an oppositional stance against the CPP. For instance, the President of FUNCINPEC, Prince Norodom Ranariddh, said on the 2018 campaign trail that "If you don't like me vote for the CPP" (Pou, 23 July 2018).

Leading up to the 2018 elections, the CPP was concerned about the legitimacy of the election, particularly if voter turnout dropped. The banned CNRP called for a popular boycott of the elections. In response to this appeal, the CPP launched a nation-wide campaign to drive out voters. While curtailing worker protest, Prime Minister Hun Sen launched a campaign to influence workers' electoral choice through gift-giving and policy actions to increase workers' wages and benefits. The government, according to CPP apparatchiks, attempted to achieve two objectives. First, as the aforementioned discussion shows, workers have influence over their family members. So winning over workers' support might lead to winning over support from their family members as well.[34] Second, CPP attempts to co-opt workers prevented them from organizing demonstrations.

---

[34] Author's field-note, June-July, 2018.

Reports also surfaced that in rural areas CPP agents threatened voters that the party has the "eyes like a pineapple"[35] and would instantly know who boycotted the elections. CPP dominated local authorities also threatened to deny services such as the issuance of birth certificates and the transfer of property titles to those who boycotted the poll. Government employees faced threats of potential discrimination if they failed to vote. In some areas in rural Cambodia, sticking to its old habits, the CPP offered financial inducements of US$5 dollars to voters, with a promise of an additional US$5 dollars with proof of voting by showing their inked index figure.[36] In past elections, the government did what it could to discourage workers from travelling to vote in their home villages. In contrast, during the elections in 2018, the government instructed businesses including garment factories to allow voters to take paid leave to travel to their home village to vote. The CPP warned against those who incited people to boycott the poll with stiff fines of between US$1,250 and $5,000 (Radio Free Asia, 2018).

In the elections held on July 29, 2018, the CPP captured 77.5 per cent of the votes cast and all 125 seats of the National Assembly, shutting out the remaining 19 parties (NEC, 2018). According to official figures, voter turnout was 82 percent (NEC, 2018) higher than that of the 2013 election, which was at 69.6 percent rate (COMFREL, 2013). The banned CNRP disputed these high turnout figures alleging distortion by NEC. These allegations notwithstanding, the level of ballot-spoiling was also high, at over 9 percent compared with just over 1 percent in 2013. It should be noted that the 2018 election had only 8.38 million registered voters compared to 9.68 million in 2013. The lower number of people who registered to vote and the higher number of spoiled ballots could well be signs of voter dissatisfaction with the process.

6.2 China: The Enabling Factor

Many news reports and commentaries seem to suggest that China's assistance to, investment in, and trade with Cambodia are to blame for Cambodia's return to authoritarianism. This view does not fully capture the CPP's decision. The CPP would have shut down the democratic process if its grip on power was threatened with or without China's engagement. The CPP's action to ban the CNRP had its precedent when the party was concerned in 1996–1997 that FUNCINPEC might form a military alliance with the remnants of the Khmer Rouge – an alliance that could tip the balance of power in favor of

---

[35] A phrase used by the Khmer Rouge during its rule (1975–1979).

[36] Author's field notes, June-July 2018.

FUNCINPEC. Furthermore, the CPP feared that an electoral defeat would result in societal revenge against its political and economic interests. The CPP in general, and Prime Minister Hun Sen in particular, have a sense of ownership over Cambodia, as they were the ones who liberated Cambodia from the ghastly Khmer Rouge regime and rebuilt the country in the face of the Western embargo in the 1980s. In short, the CPP likely would have decided to strike the CNRP with or without China's engagement because the CNRP had become an existential threat to the CPP (D4, July 14, 2018). However, it should be noted that China's engagement in Cambodia served as an important enabling factor for the CPP as Chinese aid and investment help to mitigate the economic and diplomatic cost of the CPP's action to return Cambodia to authoritarianism.

Since Cambodia's democracy is a product of Western intervention and engagement, Western donors have wanted to see at least some semblance of democracy, including the presence of a genuine opposition party. In the midst of the assault on the opposition, the media, and civil society, Western governments issued critical statements warning the Cambodian government of consequences. The European Union warned of the possible loss of preferential access to the EU market through the aforementioned "Everything But Arms" trade scheme if the CPP failed to restore genuine multi-party democracy in Cambodia. The US government adopted policies of targeted sanctions, which included freezing the assets of and denying visas to the United States to Cambodian government officials who were closely involved with shutting down democracy in Cambodia (Foreign Affairs Committee, US Congress, 2018). On the contrary, in response to Kem's arrest, the Chinese government stated that "the Chinese side has always supported . . . the Cambodian government's efforts to uphold national security and stability" (Ministry of Foreign Affairs of the People Republic of China, 2017).

The Cambodian government wanted to obtain international endorsement of the 2018 elections. Major Western governments such as the United States, and the European Union, however, distanced themselves from the electoral process by withdrawing their financial support to the NEC and by refusing to send election observers to Cambodia. In contrast, the Chinese government offered financial assistance to the NEC and sent a large contingent of election observers to Cambodia (Chen, 2017). Chinese delegates in fact constituted the majority of the international observers who came mainly from non-democratic countries. Furthermore, the United States and the EU condemned elections as lacking credibility. As expected, China endorsed the outcome. The Chinese government praised the NEC for its professional conduct, viewed the elections result as an indication of the Cambodian people's "affirmation and trust in the CPP" and vowed to provide resolute support for "Cambodia's efforts to protect its sovereignty, independence and stability, and oppose any foreign country interfering in Cambodia's internal affairs" (Blanchard, 2018).

It is important to note that China's engagement in Cambodia will also help to stabilize the country's authoritarian rule. While the governments of both Cambodia and China insist that China's aid is based on "the principles of non-interference," it is clear that China's aid helps to maintain the status quo in Cambodia. China's involvement has helped the ruling CPP to strengthen its political control in critical ways, such as enhancing its performance-based legitimacy and strengthening its patronage politics and its coercive capacity. Chinese firms investing in key sectors such as agro-business and hydroelectricity often form joint ventures with Cambodian business tycoons (Middleton, 2008; Barney, 2005; Global Witness, 2007). Through joint ventures, these Chinese firms have strengthened the financial positions of Cambodian tycoons and therefore the ruling CPP given the symbiotic relation between the two entities.

The presence of Chinese companies in Cambodia also helped to bolster the CPP's coercive capacity. As a way to secure loyalty from the armed forces, in 2010 the government publicly encouraged private businesses to form relationships with security forces through which the former provide the latter with material and financial assistance (Phorn and Wallace, 2010). The private company–military relationship was reportedly extended to Chinese firms. For example, a major Chinese investment company, the Union Group, was reported to have formed a "military–commercial alliance" with the Prime Minister's Bodyguard Unit (BHQ), through which the Union Group expected to provide military assistance to the unit (Kynge, Haddou, and Peel, 2016). Furthermore, the Chinese government has also provided financial support and material assistance to the Cambodian armed forces, which has strengthened their coercive capacity. In 2018 the Chinese military held a joint military exercise, dubbed "the Golden Dragon," involving Brigade 70, which is a reserve Unit of Prime Minister Hun Sen's BHQ. In preparing for the joint exercise, Brigade 70 received tanks and other military equipment from its Chinese counterparts. The BHQ, as noted above, is the backbone of Prime Minister Hun Sen's power.

This section shows that since the United Nations imposed multi-party democracy in 1993, the incumbent CPP has used a wide variety of strategies – intimidation, violence, material inducements, and legally engineered convictions – to maintain its domination. The CPP's level of deployment of authoritarian measures has shifted over time, contingent upon the level of competiveness posed by the opposition parties and the appeal of its patronage handouts. When the opposition camp was divided, and thus its level of competitiveness was manageable, the CPP allowed rather more competitive elections to occur. However, following over a decade of economic growth, and faced with social and demographic change, a unified opposition, increased popular political awareness and demand for leadership change, the CNRP became a clear and present danger. The possibility of losing the 2018 elections was high. As a result, the CPP resorted to authoritarian measures, suppressing freedom of expression and civil society activities, eliminating the CNRP and organizing the general elections without the presence of any credible opposition party.

The Western community voiced their disproval of the return to authoritarianism in Cambodia and has taken some actions toward the CPP government. However, the Western community's actions do not have significant impact on the CPP because the latter can rely on China for trade, investment, and financial assistance.

7 Will the Pendulum Swing?

Cambodia's current democratic process began under the framework of the 1991 Paris Peace Agreement (PPA) brokered plan in an era of Western euphoria over the perceived preeminence of liberal democracy and market economics.[37] International intervention can attempt to impose democracy on a war-torn formerly communist, poverty-stricken country like Cambodia. However, as this Element explains, subsequent democratic development is contingent on that country's socio-economic and political conditions at the time of democratic imposition and subsequent internal and geo-political changes. International intervention did not break the neo-patrimonial nature of the Cambodian state under Cambodian People's Party (CPP) control. Rather, the incorporation of former warring factions into the CPP-dominated state intensified patronage-based politics that influenced patterns of state governance and electoral processes.

The CPP's power structure has been based on patron–client networks. Patronage politics is closely bound to corruption for two fundamental reasons. Part of the resources generated through rent-seeking go to the elites' personal aggrandizement and to fund the CPP's electoral patronage. Patronage sustained by corruption dominates state institutions and weakens their capacity to mobilize resources for public service provision. Although

---

[37] See for example, Fukuyama (1989).

the state is weak in administrative capacity, it is strong in coercive capacity.

Since the security forces and the judiciary are woven into a net of neo-patrimonialism, subject to executive manipulation and infected by corruption and favoritism, three critical consequences follow. First, elites use these coercive institutions to promote and protect their economic interests often at the expense of the poor. Second, the government persistently uses these institutions to promote "rule by law" – a euphemism for selective application of the law by a politicized judiciary – to suppress its opponents. And third, the government takes only cosmetic action toward institutional reforms.

Institutional weakness compounded by low levels of economic development limit the state capacity to mobilize resources for the public good. Consequently, the Cambodian state has relied on international financial assistance for its development projects. Such reliance has allowed the Western community to pressure Cambodia to maintain at least some semblance of democracy. As long as such political order permitted the CPP to maintain its domination, it conceded to Western demands. The CPP has relied on patronage, in addition to the now less frequently employed intimidation and violence, to perpetuate its political domination under electoral authoritarianism. For approximately fifteen years leading up to the 2013 elections, given the divisions within the opposition, Cambodia's low level of socio-economic development and the lack of social mobilization, the CPP could rely on generating support through patronage handouts delivered by the party working groups (PWG) to rural communities. These political machines embodied a symbiotic relationship between state institutions, party officials, and business tycoons. They dispensed resources across Cambodia's countryside constructing roads, irrigation networks, and schools. Through these "development projects," the CPP has projected itself as an indispensable force for Cambodia's economic progress and political stability.

However, by the 2013 elections, key socio-economic and political changes occurred which culminated in a counter-movement to the CPP. First, economic development and concomitant urbanization and widespread access to communication and information technology generated broad social and political consciousness among the populace. The growth of the garment industry and national and international migration to engage in wage labor spawned a progressive labor force. Not only did the majority of migrants support the opposition party, these workers – through the power of their remittances – also influenced their families' political views. Their experiences living abroad and in the city expanded their vistas and attitudes toward change and modernization. Moreover, the expansion of affordable telecommunications made possible extensive use of social media allowing Cambodians to access, discuss, and share information. These exchanges had political spillover effects. First, the exchange of information undermined the CPP's monopoly over traditional media platforms permitting the opposition parties and civil society organizations (CSOs) to have direct contact with the Cambodian electorate. Second, the exchange of information made possible the nationwide exposure of local resource expropriation by networks of crony-tycoons highlighting the negative effects of the CPP's patronage politics and therefore undermining the CPP's legitimacy.

Around the same time, Cambodian civil society was also transformed. It had been dominated by non-governmental organizations (NGOs) whose work largely focused on the provision of services and education on human rights and democracy. By the early 2000s, key developments transformed the landscape of Cambodian society. First, political decentralization opened political space for popular engagement in local affairs. Second, crony-based expropriation of natural resources affected many lives in rural Cambodia. These developments drove many villagers to form community-based organizations (CBOs) to protect themselves from the ravages of crony-capitalism. With assistance from international NGOs and Western bilateral aid agencies, Cambodian NGOs increased contact with local people, aiding them in nurturing CBOs. The opposition camp capitalized on these social transformation through the formation of a united opposition party (Cambodia National Rescue Party, CNRP), creating a counter-movement to CPP domination, culminating in a credible CNRP electoral threat in the 2013 and 2017 elections.

As this Element suggests, the CPP was always suspicious, if not fearful, that liberal democracy could take root in Cambodia. When the CPP felt that its grip on power was threatened, it took autocratic measures including using military force to weaken National United Front for an Independent, Neutral, Peaceful and Cooperative Cambodia (FUNCINPEC) in 1997, and deploying the politicized judiciary to dismantle the CNRP and clamping down on the press and civil society following the 2017 local elections. Since Cambodia's democracy is, in large part, a product of Western intervention and engagement in the form of leverage through trade and development assistance, Cambodia's recent return to authoritarianism can to some extent be attributed to shifting global geo-politics. Since around 2000, Cambodia has pivoted to China, which has become Cambodia's leading trade partner and donor. Increasingly, China's assistance to Cambodia has offered Cambodia counter-leverage to Western pressure to maintain some semblance of democracy. In this case, China looms large and serves as an enabling factor in the CPP's return of Cambodia to authoritarianism, cushioning the consequences of an economic backlash resulting from potential Western economic sanctions. The EU has in 2018 issued an ultimatum for the Cambodian government to restore democracy and the respect for human rights or face EU's suspension of Cambodia's preferential trade status under the "Everything But Arms" scheme. If China's aid, investment, and trade cannot cover the loss associated with EU's sanctions, then the electoral authoritarian pendulum can swing back, though it is unlikely to reach pre-2017 levels. The CPP will likely allow the opposition CNRP to reconstitute in new form, though it will ban it again when the next election cycle comes. If China's aid, investment, and trade are sufficient to permit the CPP to ignore the EU's pressure, the CPP's challenge is to meet the heightened popular desire for a state with the capacity to respond to their material needs. These actions require that the CPP strengthen state capacity. Effective reform is a challenge given still pervasive neo-patrimonialism. Ongoing economic growth, the CPP's complete control over the security forces, and the windfall of China's aid and investment, mean that the CPP will be able to diffuse any potential societal pressure at least into the intermediate future.

References

Book, Articles, and Reports

Arnold, D. (2017). Civil Society, Political Society, and Politics of Disorder in Cambodia. *Political Geography*, (60): 23–33.

Asia Foundation (2003). Democracy in Cambodia 2003: A Survey of the Cambodian Electorate. Available at: https://asiafoundation.org/resources/pdfs/DemocracyinCambodia.pdf (accessed April 1, 2018).

Barber, J. and Chaumau, C. (1997). Slaughter on Sunday – March 30, 1997. *The Phnom Penh Post*, April 4–17.

BBC World Service Trust (2010). *Youth Civic Participation in Cambodia: Knowledge, Attitudes, Practices, and Media*. Phnom Penh: United Nations Development Programme in Cambodia.

Barney, K. (2005). "Customs, Concessionaires, Conflict: Tracking Cambodia's Forest Commodity Chains and Export Links With China." *Forest Trends*, 2005. Available at: www.foresttrends.org/documents/publications/Cambodia%20Report%20New.pdf (accessed April 30, 2009).

Beban, A., So, S., and Un, K. (2017). From Force to Legitimation: Rethinking Land Grabs in Cambodia. *Development and Change*, 48(3), 590–612.

Bessant, D. (2014). A Fistful of Donors. *Southeast Asia Globe*, 16 January. Available at: http://sea-globe.com/ngos-in-cambodia (accessed October 18, 2017).

Bjornlund, E. (2001). Democracy Inc. *The Wilson Quarterly*, 25(3),18–24.

Blanchard, B. (2018). China Says Foreigners Should Not Interfere in Cambodia after Election. *Reuter*, August 1. Available at: www.reuters.com/article/us-asean-singapore-china-cambodia/china-says-foreigners-should-not-interfere-in-cambodia-after-election-idUSKBN1KN034 (access August 9, 2018).

Bopha, P. and Wallace, J. (2010). Businesses Tie Official Knot With Military. *The Cambodia Daily*, February 26.

The Cambodia Daily (2002). Hun Sen Says Khmer Rouge Trial "a Must." June 3.

Cambodia Development Resource Institute and Asian Development Bank (2000). *Cambodia: Enhancing Governance for Sustainable Development*, Final Report (Unedited Version). Presented to the Royal Government of Cambodia, Phnom Penh, April 2000. Phnom Penh: Asian Development-Cambodia.

Cambodia Development Resource Institute (2018). *A Survey of Cambodian Citizens on Family and Community Relations, Political Attitudes, Life Priorities, and Future Expectations.* Phnom Penh: Cambodia Development Resource Institute.

Center for Social Development (1998). *National Survey on Public Attitudes Towards Corruption: Summery Report.* Phnom Penh: Center for Social Development.

Central Intelligence Agency (n.d.). East and Southeast Asia: Cambodia. Available at: www.cia.gov/library/publications/the-world-factbook/geos/cb.html (accessed May 17, 2014).

Chabal, P. and Daloz, J. P. (1999). *Africa Works: Disorder as Political Instrument.* Indiana: Indiana University Press.

Chanda, N. (1986). *Brother Enemy: The War after the War.* New York: Harcourt.

(2002). China and Cambodia: In the Mirror of History. *Asia Pacific Review* 9(2),1–11.

Chandler, D. (1991). *The Tragedy of Cambodian History: Politics, War, and Revolution Since 1945.* New Haven: Yale University Press.

(1998). The Burden of Cambodia's Past. In F. Z. Brown and D. G. Timberman, eds., *Cambodia and the International Community: The Quest for Peace, Development, and Democracy.* New York and Singapore: Asia Society and Institute of Southeast Asian Studies, pp. 33–48.

(2008). *A History of Cambodia*, 4th Edition. Boulder: Westview Press.

Cheang, S. (2017). Envoy Who Cares about Workers in South Korea. *Khmer Times*, November 16. Available at: www.khmertimeskh.com/5090717/envoy-cares-workers-korea (accessed August 14, 2018).

Chen, Daphne. (2017). *Following US, EU Withdrawal of Funding, China to Donate Huge Load of Goods to NEC.* Phnom Penh Post, December 29. Available at: www.phnompenhpost.com/national/following-us-eu-withdrawal-funding-china-donate-huge-load-goods-nec (accessed October 4, 2018).

Clean Clothes Campaign (2015). *Cambodian Trade Unions Sidelined in Preparation of Draft Trade Union Law.* Available at: https://cleanclothes.org/news/2015/10/09/cambodia-trade-unions-sidelined-in-preparations-of-draft-trade-union-law (accessed September 12, 2018).

Cochrane, L. (2007). Cambodia: Can't See the Forest for the Thieves. *World Politics Review*, 06 June. Available at: www.worldpoliticsreview.com/article.aspx?id=829 (accessed September 15, 2018).

COMFREL (2013). *2013 National Assembly Elections Final Assessment and Report.* Available at: www.comfrel.org/eng/components/com_mypublica

tions/files/781389Final_Report_and_Assessment_National_Assembly_Ele ctions_Final_24_12_2013.pdf (accessed August 10, 2018).

(2017). Final Assessment and Report: the 2017 Commune Council Election. Available at: https://comfrel.org/english/final-assessment-and-report-the-2017-commune-council-eelection (accessed October 11, 2018).

Constitution of the Kingdom of Cambodia (1993). Available at: www.wipo.int/ edocs/lexdocs/laws/en/kh/kh009en.pdf. (accessed September 15, 2018).

Cooperation Committee for Cambodia (2010). *Reflections, Challenges, and Choices: 2010 Review of NGO Sector in Cambodia*. Phnom Penh: Cooperation Committee for Cambodia.

(2012). *CSO Contributions to the Development of Cambodia 2012: Opportunities and Challenges*. Available at: www.ccc-cambodia.org/back end/web/uploads/resource/media/CSO_Contributions_Report_2012_EN-58ba7ab272a44.pdf (accessed October 16, 2017).

Croissant, A. (2016). *Electoral Politics in Cambodia: Historical Trajectories, Current Challenges, and Comparative Perspectives*. Konrad Adenauer Stiftung. Available at: www.kas.de/wf/doc/kas_46876–544-1-30.pdf? 161102083353 (accessed October 7, 2017).

Dapice, D. (2005). *A SWOT Analysis of Cambodia*. Phnom Penh: United Nations Development Programme.

Diamond, L. (2002). Thinking About Hybrid Regimes. *Journal of Democracy*, 13(2), 21–35.

Donovan, D. A. (1993). The Cambodian Legal System: An Overview. In F. Brown, ed., *Rebuilding Cambodia: Human Resources, Human Rights, and Law*. Washington: Foreign Policy Institute, Paul H. Nitze School of Advanced International Studies, John Hopkins University, pp. 60–107.

Dreher, A., Fuchs, A., Parks, B. C., Strange, A. M., and Tierney, M. J. (2017). *Aid, China, and Growth: Evidence from a New Global Development Finance Dataset*. AidData Working Paper #46. Williamsburg, VA: AidData. Available at: www.aiddata.org/publications/aid-china-and-growth-evidence-from-a-new-global-development-finance-dataset (accessed September 13, 2018).

Ebihara, M. (2018). *Svay, A Khmer Village in Cambodia*. Ithaca: Cornell University Press.

Eisenstadt, S. and Roniger, L. (1984). *Patrons, Clients and Friends: Interpersonal Relations and the Structure of Trust in Society*. Cambridge University Press.

Ellis-Petersen. H. (2018). No Cambodia Left: How Chinese Money is Changing Sihanoukville. *The Guardian*, 31 July. Available at:

www.theguardian.com/cities/2018/jul/31/no-cambodia-left-chinese-money-changing-sihanoukville (accessed August 15, 2018).

Eng, N. (2014). The Politics of Decentralisation in Cambodia: the District Level. PhD Dissertation, School of Politics and Social Inquiry, Monash University.

Eng, N. and Ear, S. (2016). Decentralization Reforms in Cambodia. *Journal of Southeast Asian Economies*, 33(2), 209–223.

Everett, S. and Meisburger, T. (2014). *Democracy in Cambodia 2014: A Survey of the Cambodian Electorate*. Phnom Penh: The Asia Foundation. Available at: https://asiafoundation.org/resources/pdfs/DemocracyinCambodia2014.pdf (accessed February 20, 2018).

Extraordinary Chambers in the Courts of Cambodia. Available at: www.eccc.gov.kh/en/node/39457 (accessed October 10, 2018).

Far Eastern Economic Review (1993a). Bitter Victory: Poll Winners Find It Hard to Grasp Levers of Power. December 9.

(1993b). Concentrating the Mind. December 30.

(1994). Center Cannot Hold: Sihanouk Fears For the Future of His Country. May 19.

Ford, M. and Gillan., M. (2017). In Search of a Living Wage in Southeast Asia. *Employee Relations*, 39(6), 903–914.

Foreign Affairs Committee, the United States House of Representative (2018). Press Release: House Passes Cambodia Democracy Act. 25 July. Available at: https://foreignaffairs.house.gov/press-release/house-passes-cambodia-democracy-act (accessed August 15, 2018).

Frieson, K. (1996). The Politics of Getting the Voter. In S. Heder and J. Ledgerwood, eds., *Propaganda, Politics and Violence in Cambodia: Democratic Transition under United Nations Peace-Keeping*. Armonk: M.E. Sharpe, pp. 183–207.

Fukuyama, F. (1989). The End of History? *The National Interest*, 16, 3–18.

Global Witness. (1998). *Country for Sale: How Cambodia's Elite Has Captured the Country's Extractive Industries*. Available at: www.globalwitness.org/en/reports/country-sale (accessed October 15, 2017).

(2007). *Cambodia's Family Trees: Illegal Logging and the Stripping of Public Assets by Cambodia's Elite*. Available at: www.globalwitness.org/en/reports/cambodias-family-trees (accessed December 30, 2017).

(2013). *Rubber Barons: How Vietnamese Companies and International Financiers Are Driving a Land Grabbing Crisis in Cambodia and Laos*. Available at: www.globalwitness.org/sites/default/files/library/Rubber_Barons_lores_0.pdf (accessed December 20, 2018).

Gottesman, E. (2003). *Cambodia after the Khmer Rouge: Inside the Politics of Nation Building*. New Haven: Yale University Press.

Heder, S. (1995). Cambodia's Democratic Transition to Neoauthoritarianism. *Current History*, 94, 425–429.

(2005). Hun Sen's Consolidation of Power: The Death or Beginning of Reform. *Southeast Asian Affairs*, 1, 111–130.

Heder, S and Ledgerwood, J. eds. (1996). *Propaganda, Politics and Violence: Democratic Transition under United Nations Peace-keeping*. New York: ME Sharpe.

Hideyuki A. (2003). *Cambodia General Election 2003: Report of International Observation Mission*. Bangkok: Asian Network for Free Elections (ANFREL) and Asian Forum for Human Rights and Development.

Holmes, O. (2017). "Death of Democracy" in Cambodia as Court Dissolves Opposition. *The Guardian*. Available at: www.theguardian.com/world/ 2017/nov/16/death-of-democracy-cambodia-court-dissolves-opposition-hun-sen (accessed February 3, 2018).

(2001). Mystics and Militants: Democratic Reform in Cambodia. *International Politics*, 38(1),47–64.

(2003). *The Political Economy of Cambodia's Transition, 1991–2001*. Richmond: Routledge Curzon.

(2006). The Politics of Gifts: Tradition and Regimentation in Contemporary Cambodia. *Journal of Southeast Asian Studies*, 37(3), 469–489.

(2007). Transnational Networks, International Organizations and Political Participation in Cambodia: Human Rights, Labour Rights and Common Rights. *Democratization*, 14(5), 834–852.

(2009). *Dependent Communities: Aid and Politics in Cambodia and East Timor*. Ithaca: Cornell University Press.

(2013). "Understanding the Elections in Cambodia 2013," *AGLOS: Journal of Area- Based Global Studies*. AGLOS Special Issue: Workshop and Symposium 2013–2014. Available at: http://dept.sophia.ac.jp/g/gs/wpcon tent/uploads/2015/06/b98c8184d35f9b156df22f210dd322a2.pdf (accessed September 12, 2018).

Hughes, C. and Real, S. (2000). *Nature of Causes of Conflict Escalation in the 1998 National Election*. Phnom Penh: Cambodian Development Resource Institute-Cambodian Center for Conflict Resolution.

Hughes, C. and Un, K. (2007). *Cambodia Country Governance Analysis*. Phnom Penh: DFID, Embassy of the United Kingdom.

Hughes, C. and Un, K., eds. (2011b). Cambodia's Economic Transformation: Historical and Theoretical Frameworks. In Hughes, C. and Un, K., eds., *Cambodia's Economic Transformation*. Copenhagen: Nordic Institute of Asian Studies, pp. 1–26.

Human Rights Watch (2009). *Cambodia: 1997 Grenade Attack on Opposition Still Unpunished: Suspects in Attack Have Been Promoted Instead of Prosecuted.* Available at: www.hrw.org/news/2009/03/30/cambodia-1997-grenade-attack-opposition-still-unpunished (accessed September 2, 2015).

Hun Sen, Facebook (accessed August10, 2018).

Huntington, S. (1996). *Political Order in Changing Societies.* New Haven: Yale University Press.

International Center for Non-Profit Law (2018). Civic Monitor: Cambodia. Available at: www.icnl.org/research/monitor/cambodia.html (accessed October 11, 2018).

International Republican Institute (IRI). *Survey of Cambodian Public Opinion* 2007, 2009, 2010, 2011, 2012, 2013, 2014. Available at: www.iri.org/news-and-resource?type=1&country=670 (accessed January 10, 2018).

Kato, T. (2000). *Cambodia Enhancing Governance for Sustainable Development.* Phnom Penh: Asian Development Bank and Cambodian Development Resource Institute.

Kaufmann, D. and Kraay, A. (2016). *Worldwide Governance Indicators. World Bank.* Available from: http://info.worldbank.org/governance/wgi/#home (accessed December 26, 2017).

Khy, S. (2017). Court "Must Solve" Corruption Conundrum. *The Cambodia Daily*, 20 June.

Kiernan, B. (2002). *The Pol Pot Regime: Race, Power, and Genocide in Cambodia Under the Khmer* Rouge, *1975–1979.* Yale University Press.

Kyne, P. (1999). Cambodia's Kingdom of Corruption: the High Cost of Doing Business. *The Phnom Penh Post*, June 25–July 8.

Kynge, J., Haddou, L., and Peel. M. (2016). FT Investigation: How China Bought its Way into Cambodia. *Financial Times*, September 8. Available at: www.ft.com/content/23968248-43a0-11e6-b22f-79eb4891c97d (accessed April 26, 2018).

Lang, R. (1996). Trade Status Herald New Age in Cambodia-US Ties. *The Phnom Penh Post*, October 4. Available at: www.phnompenhpost.com/national/trade-status-heralds-new-age-cambodia-us-ties (accessed September 12, 2018).

Lao, M. H. (1998). Cambodia's Agonizing Quest: Political Progress amid Institutional Backwardness. In D. Hendrickson, ed., *Safeguarding Peace: Cambodia's Constitutional Challenge.* London: Conciliation Resources, pp. 36–42.

(2006). "Institutions for the Rule of Law and Human Rights in Cambodia." Available at: http://alrc.asia/article2/2006/02/institutions-for-the-rule-of-law-and-human-rights-in-cambodia (accessed September 07, 2018).

Laws Associations and Non-governmental Organizations (Unofficial Translation by OHCHR of the Law Approved by National Assembly on July 13, 2015). Available at: http://cambodia.ohchr.org/~cambodiaohchr/sites/default/files/Unofficial_Translation_of_5th_LANGO_ENG.pdf (accessed April 1, 2018).

Le Billon, P. (2002). Logging in Muddy Waters: The Politics of Forest Exploitation in Cambodia. *Critical Asian Studies*, 34(4), 563–586.

Ledgerwood, J. and Un, K. (2003). Global Concepts and Local Meaning: Human Rights and Buddhism in Cambodia. *Journal of Human Rights*, 2(4), 531–549.

Leifer, M. (1968). The Failure of Political Institutionalization in Cambodia. *Modern Asian Studies*, 2(2), 125–140.

Lemarchand, R. (1988). The State, the Parallel Economy and the Changing Structure of Patronage Politics. In D. Rothchild and N. Chazan, eds., *The Precarious Balance: State and Society in Africa*. Boulder: Westview Press, pp. 150–157.

Levitsky, S. and Way, L. (2010). *Competitive Authoritarianism: Hybrid Regimes after the Cold War*. New York: Cambridge University Press.

Lewis, S. (2012). "Japan Adds to Criticism of Cambodia's Role as ASEAN Chair", *Cambodia Daily*, September 9.

Lewis, S. and Kuch N. (2013). Constitutional Council Pivotal in Election Stalemate, *The Cambodia Daily*, 7 August. Available at: www.cambodiadaily.com/elections/constitutional-council-pivotal-in-election-stalemate-38528 (accessed December 29, 2017).

LICADO (2014). Statement: 2014 Brings a New Wave of Cambodian Land Conflicts. Available at: www.licadho-cambodia.org/pressrelease.php?perm=342 (accessed August 22, 2018).

Lum, T., Morrison, W., and Vaughn. B. (2008). China's "Soft Power" in Southeast Asia. *CRS Report for Congress*, June. Available at: www.fas.org/sgp/crs/row/RL34310.pdf (accessed March 20, 2009).

Marks, P. (2000). China's Cambodia Strategy. *Parameters Online*, Autumn 2000. Available at: www.sophanseng.info/wp-content/uploads/2015/05/Chinas-Cambodia-Strategy.pdf (accessed October 4, 2018).

May, T. (2014). Kings of Concessions. *The Phnom Penh Post*, February 25. Available at: www.phnompenhpost.com/national/kings-concessions (accessed October 4, 2014).

    (2017). China Agenda Fuels "Treason" Plot Support. *Khmer Times*, September 8. Available at: www.khmertimeskh.com/5082099/china-agenda-fuels-treason-plot-support (accessed September 9, 2017).

McCarthy, S. and Un, K. (2017). The Evolution of Rule of Law in Cambodia. *Democratization*, 24(1): 100–118.

McLeod, R. (2000). Soeharto's Indonesia: A Better Class of Corruption. *Agenda* 7(2), 99–112.

Meach, D. and Turton, S. (2017). Third Member of PM's Bodyguard Unit Seen Kicking head of MP Promoted. *The Phnom Penh Post*, January 26.

Meas, S. and Handley, E. (2017). CPP Amends Party Law, Opening Door to Dissolving Opposition. *The Phnom Penh Post*, February 21. Available at: www.phnompenhpost.com/national/cpp-amends-party-law-opening-door-dissolving-opposition (accessed February 3, 2018).

Mech, D. (2017). Generals Added Amid Political Crackdown. *The Phnom Penh Post*, November 27.

Meta, K., (2018). Migrants Face Thai Deadline. *The Phnom Penh Post*, June 20. Available at: www.phnompenhpost.com/national/migrants-face-thai-deadline (accessed October 11, 2018).

Middleton, C. (2008). *Cambodia's Hydropower Development and China's Involvement*. Berkeley: International Rivers.

Ministry of Foreign Affairs of the People's Republic of China (2017). Foreign Ministry Spokesperson Geng Shuang's Regular Press Conference on September 4, 2017. Available at: www.fmprc.gov.cn/mfa_eng/xwfw_665399/s2510_665401/t1489891.shtml (accessed October 11, 2018).

Mogato, M., Marina M., and Blanchard, S. (2016). ASEAN Deadlocked on South China Sea: Cambodia Blocks Statement. Available at: www.reuters.com/article/us-southchinasea-ruling-asean/asean-deadlocked-on-south-china-sea-cambodia-blocks-statement-idUSKCN1050F6 (accessed September 15, 2018).

Morgenbesser, L. (2017). Misclassification on the Mekong: the Origins of Hun Sen's Personalist Dictatorship," *Democratization*, 25(2), 191–208.

Kuch, N. and Seiff, A. (2012). Adhoc Rights Workers Charged with Aiding Perpetrator, *The Cambodia Daily*, August 15.

National Committee for Sub-national Democratic Development (2014). *Is Governance Improving? A Comparison of the Results of the 2011 and 2013 IP3 Governance Perception Survey*. April 6. Phnom Penh: Ministry of Interior.

National Election Committee (NEC) (2018). *News Release on the Preliminary Results of the Parliamentary Elections July 29, 2018*. Available at: www.necelect.org.kh/khmer/content/3463 (accessed August 10, 2018).

Nohlen, D., Grotz, F., and Hartmann, C. (2001). *Elections in Asia: A Data Handbook*, Volume II. Oxford University Press.

Norén-Nilsson, A. (2016a). *Cambodia's Second Kingdom: Nation, Imagination, and Democracy* Ithaca: Southeast Asia Program, Cornell University.

(2016b). Good Gifts, Bad Gifts, and Rights: Cambodian Popular Perceptions and the 2013 Elections. *Pacific Affairs*, 89(4), 795–815.

Nuon, V. and Serrano, M. (2010). *Building Unions in Cambodia: History, Challenges and Strategies*. Friedrich Ebert Stiftung. Available at: http://library.fes.de/pdf-files/bueros/singapur/07907.pdf (accessed August 10, 2018).

O'Donnell, G. (2004). Why the Rules of Law Matters. *Journal of Democracy*, 15(2), 32–46.

Ojendal, J. (2013). In Search of a Civil Society: A Negotiating State-Society Relations in Cambodia. In G. Waibel, J. Ehlert, and H. N. Feuer, eds., *Southeast Asia and the Civil Society Gaze: Scoping a Contested Concept in Cambodia and Vietnam*. Vol. 4. New York: Routledge, pp, 21–38.

Osborne, M. E. (1994). *Sihanouk: Prince of Light, Prince of Darkness*. Honolulu: University of Hawaii Press.

Ou, K. and Chheat, S. (2017). *Feasibility Study on Civil Society Fund (CSF) in Cambodia*. Phnom Penh: Committee for Cooperation Cambodia.

Ou, S. and Kim, S. (2013). *20 Years' Strengthening of Cambodian Civil Society: Time for Reflection*. Working Paper Series No. 85. Phnom Penh: Cambodia Development Research Institute.

PACT-Cambodia (2010). *Corruption and Cambodian Households*. Available at: www.pactcambodia.org/Publications/Anti_Corruption/Corruption&; Cambodian%20Households%202010%20Eng.pdf (accessed September 15, 2018).

Pak, K. and Craig, D. (2011). Learning from Party Financing of Local Investment Projects in Cambodia: Elite and Mass Patronage, Accountability and Decentralized Governance. In C. Hughes and K. Un, eds., *Reform and Transformation in Cambodia*. Copenhagen: NIAS, pp, 219–249.

Parameswaran, P. (2018). China-Cambodia Defense Ties in the Spotlight with Military Drills. *The Diplomat*, March 21. Available at: https://thediplomat.com/2018/03/china-cambodia-defense-ties-in-the-spotlight-with-military-drills (accessed April 26, 2018).

Peou, S. (1998). Cambodia in 1997: Back to Square One? *Asian Survey*, 38(1), 69–74.

(2001a). Pre-emptive Coup: Causes and Consequences. In S. Peou, ed., *Cambodia: Change and Continuity in Contemporary Politics*. Singapore: Ashgate, pp. 86–102.

(2001b). Cambodia after the Killing Fields. In J. Funston, ed., *Government and Politics in Southeast Asia*. Singapore: Institute of Southeast Asian Studies, pp, 36–73.

Phong, K., Srun, L., and Sola, J. (2016).*Mobile Phones and Internet Use in Cambodia 2016*. Phnom Penh:Asia Foundation. Available at: https://asia foundation.org/publication/mobile-phones-internet-use-cambodia-2016 (accessed February 3, 2018).

Phorn B., and Wallace, J. (2010). Businesses Tie Official Knot with Military. *The Cambodia Daily*, February 26.

Ponniah K. (2013). Political Eyes on Youth Voting. *The Phnom Penh Post*, July 9. Available at: www.phnompenhpost.com/national/political-eyes-youth-vote (accessed September 12, 2018).

Putnam, R., Leonardi, R. and Nanetti, R. Y. (1994). *Making Democracy Work: Civic Traditions in Modern Italy*. Princeton University Press.

Press OCM (2017). Did Color Revolution Modelling on Color Revolutions In Other Countries Around the World Really Happen in Cambodia. Phnom Penh: Royal Government of Cambodia. Available at: www .youtube.com/watch?v=3PU2RHBEQK8 (accessed October 4, 2018).

Radio Free Asia (2014). Cambodian PM Promotes 29 to Four Star General. Available at: www.rfa.org/english/news/cambodia/promotion-02052014165509.html (accessed September 2, 2015).

(2015). Cambodia's Armed Forces "Belong" to the Ruling Party. July 29. Available at: www.rfa.org/english/news/cambodia/military-072920151458 55.html (accessed September 2, 2015).

(2018). Cambodia Investigating Former Opposition Members Over Election Boycott Campaign. July 23. Available at: www.rfa.org/english/news/cam bodia/investigation-07232018165842.html (accessed August 15, 2018).

Reuters, (2018). Japan, Cambodia Sign $90 Million Aid Agreement, April 8. Available at: www.reuters.com/article/us-cambodia-japan/japan-cambo dia-sign-90-million-aid-agreement-idUSKBN1HF062 (access April 29, 2018).

Rollet, C. and Baliga, A. (2015). Too Many Unions: Owners. *The Phnom Penh Post*, September 3. Available at: www.phnompenhpost.com/business/too-many-unions-owners (accessed October 6, 2018).

Roum Rik (pseud.) (2003). On Behalf of the Pagoda Boys' Association Phnom Penh. *Phnom Penh Post*, May 9.

Rusten, C., Kim, S., Eng, N., and Pak, K. (2004). *The Challenges of Decentralisation Design in Cambodia*. Phnom Penh: Cambodia Development Resource Institute.

Salamon, L. M. (1994). The Rise of the Nonprofit Sector. *Foreign Affairs* 73 (July/August), 109–122.

Schedler, A. ed. (2006). *Electoral Authoritarianism: The Dynamics of Unfree Competition*. Boulder: Rienner.

Shawcross, W. (1981). *Sideshow: Kissinger, Nixon, and the Destruction of Cambodia*. New York: Simon & Schuster.

(1994). *Cambodia's New Deal*. Washington, D.C.: Carnegie Endowment for International Peace.

Sidel, J. (1997). Philippine Politics in Town, District, and Province: Bossism in Cavite and Cebu. *The Journal of Asian Studies*, 56(4), 947–966.

Sloth, C., Khlok, B., and Heov, K. S. (2005). Non-Timber Forest Products: Their Values to Rural Livelihood. *Cambodia Development Review*, 9(4), 1–5.

SPK (1993). Statement of the His Excellency Hun Sen to Fellow Citizens. June 13. (Author's Translation).

Spiess, R. (2018). A Sector Too Big To Fail? *Phnom Penh Post*, 5 April. Available at: www.phnompenhpost.com/business/sector-too-big-fail (accessed August 18, 2018).

Stokes, S. (2005). Perverse Accountability: A Formal Model of Machine Politics with Evidence from Argentina. *American Political Science Review*, 99(3), 315–325.

The Economist (2017). "The Giant's Client: Why Cambodia Has Cosied up To China. January 17. Available at: www.economist.com/news/asia/21715010-and-why-it-worries-cambodias-neighbours-why-cambodia-has-cosied-up-china (accessed April 1, 2018).

The Phnom Penh Post Staff (2007). Son Soubert Still Serving after 30 Years. *The Phnom Penh Post*, November 16–29. Available at: www.phnompenhpost.com/national/son-soubert-still-serving-after-30-years (accessed October 10, 2018).

Thun, V. (2014). Youth Political Participation in Cambodia: Role of Information and Communication Technologies (ICTs). Master Thesis, Northern Illinois University.

Transparency International (2007). *Global Corruption Report 2007: Corruption in Judicial Systems*. Cambridge University Press.

Un, K. (2005). Patronage Politics and Hybrid Democracy: Political Change in Cambodia, 1993–2003. *Asian Perspective*, 29(2), 203–230.

(2006). State, Society and Democratic Consolidation: The Case of Cambodia. *Pacific Affairs*, 79(2), 225–245.

(2008a). Cambodia's 2008 Parliamentary Elections: Prospects for Opposition Politics. *AsiaPacific Bulletin*, East-West Center. Available at: www.eastwestcenter.org/publications/cambodias-2008-parliamentary-elections-prospects-opposition-politics (accessed October 4, 2018).

(2008b). Sam Rainsy and the Sam Rainsy Party: Configuring Opposition Politics in Cambodia. In J. Kane, H. Patapan, and B. Wong, eds., *Dissident Democrats. The Challenge of Democratic Leadership in Asia*. Palgrave Macmillan, pp. 105–128.

(2009). The Judicial System and Democratization in Post-Conflict Cambodia. In Joakim Ojendal and Mona Lilja, eds., Beyond Democracy in Cambodia: Political Reconstruction in a Post-Conflict Society. Copenhagen: NIAS, pp. 70–100.

(2011). Cambodia: Moving Away from Democracy? *International Political Science Review*, 32(5), 546–562.

(2013a). Cambodia in 2012: Beyond the Crossroads? *Asian Survey*, 53(1), 142–149.

(2013b). The Cambodian People Have Spoken. *The New York Times*. Available at: www.nytimes.com/2013/08/10/opinion/global/the-cambodian-people-have-spoken.html (accessed February 3, 2018).

(2015). The Cambodian People Have Spoken: Has the Cambodian People's Party Heard? In Dajit Sigh, ed., *Southeast Asian Affairs*. Institute of Southeast Asian Affairs, pp. 102–116.

Un, K., and Ledgerwood, J. (2003). Cambodia in 2002: Decentralization and its Effects on Party Politics. *Asian Survey*, *43*(1), 113–119.

Un, K. and So, S. (2011). Land rights in Cambodia: How Neopatrimonial Politics Restricts Land Policy Reform. *Pacific Affairs*, 84(2), 289–308.

UNHCHR (2007). *Economic Land Concession for Economic Purposes in Cambodia: A Human Right Perspective*. Phnom Penh: United Nations Cambodia Office of the High Commissioner for Human Rights.

Verkoren, W. and Ngin, C. (2017). Organizing against Land Grabbing in Cambodia: Exploring Missing Links. *Development and Change*, 48(6), 1336–1361.

Vickery, M. (1986). *Kampuchea: Politics, Economics, and Society*. Boulder: Lynne Reinner.

(1994). The Cambodian People's Party: Where Has It Come From, Where Is It Going? *Southeast Asian Affairs*, 102–117.

White, G. (1994). Civil Society, Democratization and Development (I): Clearing the Analytical Ground. *Democratization*, 1(2), 375–390.

Williams, S. (1999). *Review of Land Issues Literature*. Phnom Penh: Oxfam.

Working Group for an ASEAN Human Rights Mechanism (2007). *Report on the Arrest of Kem Sokha and Other Public Figures*. Available at:

www.aseanhrmech.org/nwgs/cambodia/report-on-the-arrest-of-kem-sokha.html (accessed September 23, 2018).

World Bank (2003a). *Cambodia: Enhancing Service Delivery Through Improved Resource Allocation and Institutional Reform*. Report No. 25611-KH.

(2006a). *Cambodia Halving Poverty by 2015: Poverty Assessment 2006. Cambodia World Bank Newsletter*, 4(3), 1–4.

(2007). *Cambodia Sharing Growth: Equity and Development in Cambodia Equity Report 2007*. Report No. 39809-KH.

(2016). *Country Highlights: Cambodia 2016*. Available at: www.enterprisesur veys.org/~/media/GIAWB/EnterpriseSurveys/Documents/CountryHighligh ts/Cambodia-2016.pdf (accessed September 15, 2018).

(2017a). *Net ODA Received (% of GNI)*. Available at: https://data .worldbank.org/indicator/DT.ODA.ODAT.GN.ZS (accessed December 25, 2017).

(2017b). *Net Official Development Assistance Received (Current US$)*. Available at: https://data.worldbank.org/indicator/DT.ODA.ODAT.CD (accessed December 25, 2018).

(2018). *Data*. Available at: https://data.worldbank.org/indicator (accessed August 18, 2018).

Interviews

D1, interview with author, Phnom Penh, July 10, 2003.

D7, interview with author, Phnom Penh, August 2, 2011.

D3, interview with author, Phnom Penh, October 10, 2014.

D4, interview with author, Phnom Penh, July 14, 2018.

G12, interview with author, Phnom Penh, August 1, 2013.

G20, interview with author, Phnom Penh, June 27, 2017.

Steve Heder, interview with author, Phnom Penh, July 26, 2017.

Soksan Hing, interview with author, Phnom Penh, June 20, 2014.

J23, interview with author, Phnom Penh, September 25, 2002.

J32, interview with author, Phnom Penh, June 20, 2001.

Khieu Khannariddh, Minister of the Ministry of Information, interview with the author, Phnom Penh, June 16, 2005.

N2, interview with author, Phnom Penh, May 25, 2003; July 9, 2017; July 19, 2017.

N3, interview with author, Phnom Penh, January 15, 2003.

N6, interview with author, Phnom Penh, January 20, 2003; July 4, 2017.

N7, personal communication, September 5, 2018.

N14, interview with author, Phnom Penh, January 8, 2003; January 8, 2013.

N39, interview with author, Phnom Penh, June 18, 2013; July 4, 2017; July 10, 2017.

N40, interview with author, Phnom Penh, July 18, 2017.

Sothirak Pou, Executive Director, Cambodia Institute for Peace and Cooperation, Former Secretary of State, Ministry of International Affairs and Cooperation, and former Cambodian Ambassador to Japan, interview with author, July 23, 2018.

Preap Kol, Executive Director, Transparency International Cambodia, interview with author, August 2, 2017.

Acknowledgements

Ideas in this book originated and evolved with my academic career at Northern Illinois University. I owe an immense intellectual debt to my mentors Clark Neher, Dwight King, David Chandler, and Ladd Thomas. Many friends and colleagues read drafts of this book. For this I am grateful to Steve McCarthy, John Hartman, and Kenton Clymer. I also like to thank the anonymous reviewers and the series editors Meredith Weiss and Edward Aspinall for their useful comments. My friend and supervisor Scot Schraufnagel was instrumental in accommodating my schedule allowing me to complete this book. I benefited from the support of many institutions. I would like to particularly thank Northern Illinois University and its Center for Southeast Asian Studies, the Center for Khmer Studies (Cambodia), The University of Louisville Center for Asian Democracy, American University of Phnom Penh, the Royal University of Phnom Penh, The Royal Netherlands Institute of Southeast Asian Studies and the Caribbean Studies (KITLV), and the Cambodia Development and Resource Institute.

I also wish extend my gratitude to the dozens of people in Cambodia who granted me interviews and shared with me invaluable information. Without their help and cooperation, this book would not have been possible. I also benefited from discussions and assistance from a great number of people. Although the list is long, I would particularly like to mention: Kheang Leang, So Sokbunthoeun, Kim Sedara, Keo Keriya, Pak Kimchoeun, Vong Socheata, Chan Sophal, Steve Heder, Ros Sopheap, Eng Netra, Ong Limeng, Ou Sivhuoch, Leang Un, Paul Un, and Ok Serei Sopheak.

Special thanks are of course extended to my family. My father had only elementary education while my mother is illiterate; however, they emphasized the value of education. They did their utmost, even during times of financial difficulty, to send their children to school. This book is dedicated to them. Without their commitment and determination, I would never have traveled this far intellectually. My wife, Judy, and sons, Paul and Tony, have been very supportive. Their love and encouragement made this book a reality.

Cambridge Elements $\equiv$

Politics and Society in Southeast Asia

Edward Aspinall

Australian National University

Edward Aspinall is a professor of politics at the Coral Bell School of Asia-Pacific Affairs, Australian National University. A specialist of Southeast Asia, especially Indonesia, much of his research has focused on democratisation, ethnic politics and civil society in Indonesia and, most recently, clientelism across Southeast Asia.

Meredith L. Weiss

University at Albany, SUNY

Meredith L. Weiss is Professor of Political Science at the University at Albany, SUNY. Her research addresses political mobilization and contention, the politics of identity and development, and electoral politics in Southeast Asia, with particular focus on Malaysia and Singapore.

About the series

The Elements series Politics and Society in Southeast Asia includes both country-specific and thematic studies on one of the world's most dynamic regions. Each title, written by a leading scholar of that country or theme, combines a succinct, comprehensive, up-to-date overview of debates in the scholarly literature with original analysis and a clear argument.

Cambridge Elements ≡

Politics and Society in Southeast Asia

CPSIA information can be obtained
at www.ICGtesting.com
Printed in the USA
LVHW052244281120
672930LV00012B/262

9 781108 457934